Frederick Feild Whitehurst

On the Grampian hills

Grouse and ptarmigan shooting, deer stalking, salmon and trout fishing

Frederick Feild Whitehurst

On the Grampian hills
Grouse and ptarmigan shooting, deer stalking, salmon and trout fishing

ISBN/EAN: 9783743438224

Printed in Europe, USA, Canada, Australia, Japan

Cover: Foto ©Andreas Hilbeck / pixelio.de

More available books at **www.hansebooks.com**

J. C. CORDING & CO.

19, PICCADILLY,
(Corner of Air Street)

THE ORIGINAL MAKERS OF THE

VENTILATED

WATERPROOF

COATS

FOR

RIDING,

WALKING, and

FISHING.

See "*Field*," *July* 17 and 31, 1869.

CORDING'S FISHING BOOTS
Are celebrated for their Softness.

THEIR
FISHING STOCKINGS & BROGUES
Are Unequalled.

WATERPROOFS FOR THE TROPICS
Are Guaranteed.

No Connection with any other House.

The Original Business carried on at

19, PICCADILLY, LONDON.

IMPROVED BREECHLOADERS.

Largest Stock in London.

Latest Improvements, with Hammers below Line of Sight, Compressed Steel Barrels, Choke Bore, etc.

Superior Guns, in Pairs and Sets of Three, fitted in same case, ready finished as in Stock, or made to Order.

SPECIAL PIGEON GUNS,

Of great power, Hurlingham weight, Whitworth steel tubes, marvellous pattern. Trial at our Private Shooting Grounds.

HAMMERLESS GUNS,

Further Improvements in TOP LEVER, SIDE LOCKS, SAFETY SCEARS, with Block interposing.

SECOND-HAND CENTRAL-FIRES,

BY ALL THE LEADING MAKERS.

EXCELLENT PLAIN GUNS & HAMMERLESS GUNS

At Low Prices, Ten to Fifteen Guineas.

KEEPERS' GUNS, Five Guineas and upwards.

ROOK RIFLES,

The best patterns yet introduced. Perfect accuracy, good workmanship, Five Guineas; Pistol-hand, Top-Lever, Patent Spring Ejector, etc., Six, Seven, and Eight Guineas. Fine assortment to select from.

E. M. REILLY & CO.

277 (315), Oxford St., W.; 16 (502), New Oxford St.

RUE SCRIBE, PARIS.

Sole Agents for Sharp's American Rifles.

JAMES PURDEY & SONS,
287 & 289 (late 314½), OXFORD ST., W.,
Gun and Rifle Manufacturers,

BY SPECIAL APPOINTMENT TO

Her Majesty the Queen, H.R.H. the Prince of Wales, H.M. the King of Spain, and to most of the Royal Families of Europe,

Beg to inform their Patrons that in consequence of the expiration of the lease of their old premises as above (where they have been established since early in the present century), and of the increasing demand for their manufactures, they have erected new and extensive Premises, AUDLEY HOUSE, on the site of Nos. 57 and 58, SOUTH AUDLEY STREET, W., and 85, MOUNT STREET, W., to which, when finished, they will remove, besides large factories close by.

By this means, and with an increased staff of the most skilled workmen, they will be enabled, while devoting the same experience and scrupulous care to the manufacture of their weapons which has rendered the latter so famous among the best sportsmen in all countries, to better keep pace with the extra demand which there has been for their manufactures for some time past.

Their New Patent Rebounding Hammerless Gun is for **Strength, Lightness,** and **Simplicity** of construction, **the best Hammerless Gun made.**

Extra Express Double Rifles for Deerstalking on the above principle afford great safety in having no hammers or outside bolts to be caught in stalking.

These Rifles (·400 to ·577 bore) are also made with hammers, and are the fastest and **most effective ever produced.**

The demand is still rather for Central-fire Guns **with hammers,** in which, in addition to the lightness and balance for which they are so celebrated, Messrs. PURDEY & SONS have made many improvements.

Inexpensive Rook and Rabbit Rifles on a new plan, with improved sights, with which it is possible **to hit a shilling every time at 65 yards.**

Cartridges of the best quality (for which they employ specially made cases) filled on the premises by experienced loaders, at moderate prices.

JAMES PURDEY & SONS,
287 & 289 (late 314½), OXFORD STREET, LONDON, W.

SCHULTZE GUNPOWDER.

The <u>Schultze Gunpowder has Greater Penetration</u>, with <u>Less Smoke</u>, <u>Less Fouling</u>, and <u>Less Recoil</u>, than Black Powder, and was used by all the Prize Winners at the International Meeting, 1881.

EACH CANISTER BEARS A LABEL WITH THE TRADE MARK.

THE ATTENTION OF SPORTSMEN IS SPECIALLY DIRECTED TO THE

NEW GRANULATED POWDER.

To be had Retail and in Cartridges, from most respectable Dealers, and Wholesale at the Company's Offices,

3, BUCKLERSBURY,

LONDON, E.C.

ON THE GRAMPIAN HILLS.

ON THE GRAMPIAN HILLS.

GROUSE AND PTARMIGAN SHOOTING,

DEER STALKING, SALMON AND TROUT FISHING,

And Other Sketches.

BY

FRED FEILD WHITEHURST.
(A Veteran.)
AUTHOR OF "TALLYHO," "HARKAWAY," ETC.

> On yonder mountain's purple head,
> Have ptarmigan and heath-cock bled,
> And our broad nets have swept the mere
> To furnish forth your evening cheer.—*Scott.*

LONDON:
TINSLEY BROTHERS, 8, CATHERINE ST., STRAND, W.C.
1882.

CONTENTS.

CHAPTER I.
"GOING NORTH" 9

CHAPTER II.
ON THE GRAMPIAN HILLS 15

CHAPTER III.
CLIMBING THE CAIRNWALL 23

CHAPTER IV.
LOCH NA-NEAN 33

CHAPTER V.
AMONGST THE PTARMIGAN 41

CHAPTER VI.
FAREWELL TO THE HIGHLANDS 49

CHAPTER VII.
THE BRAEMAR GATHERING 57

CHAPTER VIII.
DEER-STALKING 64

CHAPTER IX.
SALMON-FISHING 68

CHAPTER X.
HINTS ANENT HIRING MOORS 71

CHAPTER XI.
AN IMPERIAL HUNTRESS 76

CHAPTER XII.
A ROYAL STAG-HUNT 88

CHAPTER XIII.
HOUNDS AND HORSES 98

CHAPTER XIV.
SIR ROBERT HARVEY'S HARRIERS 109

CHAPTER XV.
THE ROYAL BUCKHOUNDS 115

CHAPTER XVI.
A DAY'S COURSING 123

CHAPTER XVII.
HUNTING IN A HURRICANE 130

CHAPTER XVIII.
MELTON MOWBRAY 139

CHAPTER XIX.
HUNTING AT BRIGHTON. 152

CHAPTER XX.
CUB-HUNTING 159

CHAPTER XXI.
THE HUNTING SEASON 168

CHAPTER XXII.
STAGE-COACHES OF THE PERIOD 180

CHAPTER XXIII.
BY ROAD TO BRIGHTON 191

CHAPTER XXIV.
AN AUTUMN TOUR THROUGH NORTH DEVON AND SOMERSET . 197

CHAPTER XXV.
A WINTER FAIR AT BOULOGNE 203

CHAPTER XXVI.
PICCADILLY 211

CHAPTER XXVII.
THE PARK 219

CHAPTER XXVIII.
DOWN IN DENSHIRE 225

CHAPTER XXIX.
LINES SUGGESTED BY A VISIT TO "JACK BABBAGE" AND HIS "AULD WIFE" JEAN 227

CHAPTER XXX.
THE OLD SPORTSMAN'S LAMENT 229

CHAPTER XXXI.
THE HIGHLANDS 231

CHAPTER XXXII.
DRIVING RED-DEER 234

CHAPTER XXXIII.
HUNTING IN ESSEX 241

ON THE GRAMPIAN HILLS.

INTRODUCTION.

> The precious juice the Minstrel quaffed,
> And he, emboldened by the draught,
> Looked gaily back on them and laughed.
> The cordial nectar of the bowl
> Swelled his old veins and cheered his soul;
> A lighter, livelier, prelude ran
> Ere thus his tale again began.—*Scott.*

THE approbation with which "Tallyho" and "Harkaway" were received by the public has induced me to reprint the articles which appeared in *The Daily Telegraph*, detailing particulars of the fine sport I enjoyed upon the Grampian Hills during the past season, whilst shooting grouse on the rugged moorland, and ptarmigan on the steep and stony heights of Rhidorach. Whilst attempting at the same time to give a description of the grand scenery of this part of the Highlands of Scotland, a task of no ordinary difficulty, as from the "sma hulls and muckle hulls" which vary in height up to 3700 feet, a vast panorama can be surveyed of hill and dale and wide expanse of moorland, where, to quote one of Scott's vivid descriptions of wild scenery:

> There's nothing left to fancy's guess,
> You see that all is loneliness;
> And silence aids—though those steep hills
> Send to the lake a thousand rills;
> In summer time so soft they weep,
> The sound but lulls the ear asleep.

It is not only sportsmen who are devoted to shooting that I seek to interest, but those disciples of Isaac Walton as well who delight to follow the more gentle art, by telling of swiftly-flowing streams, pellucid lochs, and countless brawling burns, the homes of the salmon and the trout.

As many of my readers, in addition to indulging in the pleasant pastimes of shooting and fishing, may take a delight in all matters appertaining to the chase, I have, following the course successfully adopted in my former publications, "Tallyho" and "Harkaway," given some sketches of hunting in the shires; telling of the doings of an Imperial huntress when in pursuit of the fox; particulars of a royal stag-hunt over the moors in Devon and Somerset; driving red-deer in Thorndon Park, with some remarks on coaching, etc., with the view of upholding the manliest and most popular of our national sports at a time when they are not unfrequently attacked by a small and effeminate minority who are ever ready

> To compound for sins they are inclined to
> By damning those they have no mind to.

CHAPTER I.

"GOING NORTH."

In pursuance of a long-existing promise that I would spend a few weeks in the Highlands, for the purpose of catching trout and salmon, shooting grouse, and stalking deer, I found myself, an evening or two since, on the platform of the North-Western Railway at Euston, with the intention of "Going North," in order to fulfil that agreeable engagement. A glance sufficed to show that I was not the only person on like pleasures bent, the platform being covered with baggage of every sort and kind, and a monster train of magnificent carriages, all labelled "Perth," drawn up, which was being rapidly though quietly loaded, the order and regularity with which the vast business at this great terminus is transacted being remarkable. Inquiring for my friends, I was shown into a new saloon carriage of improved make, the centre compartment being arranged as a sitting-room, whilst at either end were compartments, the one for the ladies, and the other for the gentlemen of the party, fitted up with comfortable beds, tastily decorated, and beautifully clean, which proved, when the hour for seeking repose at high speed arrived, eminently comfortable and conducive to rest. Lavatories of the most complete form and convenient arrangement were provided; and, in fact, this suite of rooms, which were reserved for the sole use of our party of six, comprised an amount of luxury and comfort that exhibited an entirely new feature in railway travelling, even to one not unaccustomed to locomotion on the rail. By degrees the carriages were filled up until every space was occupied in the five double saloons and nineteen first-class carriages; then the clock struck eight, and this enormous train, with a freight of 420 passengers, steamed quietly out of the station, and was soon "Going North" at express speed. It was evident that my companions were not novices in travelling; for, by a clever arrangement of some of the larger pieces of baggage, a substantial table was formed, and dinner laid for six, with little loss of time. This arrangement combined all the pleasures of a picnic with an absence of those discomforts that are usually attendant on al-fresco entertainments in this variable clime. The cold chickens, currie, fruits, and champagne partaken of whilst travelling at a speed of sixty or seventy miles an hour were even more enjoyable than similar viands consumed on the damp grass of some picturesque and romantic spot under a widely-spreading umbrella, even if the object of your affections shared the shelter of your gingham, clinging tenderly to you for protection from the inevitable thunderstorm that invariably breaks over such outdoor entertainments; for I have known even some of the fairest and most delightful of the opposite sex to become a trifle touchy under such trying circumstances.

Whilst we were dining thus luxuriously the train

was pursuing its fleet career past Harrow, through Watford, Bletchley, halting at Rugby for a while. Then away at full speed, whilst the steadiness of the carriages, even when whirling along at this rate, was the subject of discussion as being something remarkable, reflecting the highest credit on those charged with the maintenance of the road, and the construction of these ponderous vehicles, which surpass in comfort and convenience all others which I have ever met with. Having finished our cigars, and being assured that it was customary when "Going North" just to take a wee drop of whisky before going to bed, I fell in with this arrangement not unwillingly, and was soon between the snow-white sheets, dreaming that some one had sent for me in a hurry, and that I was travelling in the cabin of a first-class steamer, which, by some clever feat in engineering, had been adapted to cross the line or go on the railway track with equal facility. Occasionally a halt was made, and murmurs of "Wigan," "Carlisle," "Carstairs," broke on my drowsy and inattentive ear. I did not care; such places had no attraction for me. I was going farther North, and would wait until the welcome sound of Perth Station aroused me.

Owing to the heavy load, this train was an hour late, performing the journey, which is over 400 miles, in thirteen hours on this occasion, instead of twelve, the usual time. Perth Station was a busy scene indeed. Mountains of luggage; numbers of pointers, setters, clumbers, and those on sporting amusements bent, clad in knickerbockers and tweed suits more or less conspicuous according to the taste of the wearer. All was business; no bustle; careful, steady porters took charge of your luggage; courteous officials directed you to your carriage and supplied any required information, in such a fashion as could be followed by certain other railway companies with very great advantage to their passengers. We were bound for Blairgowrie, and had to transfer ourselves and an unknown quantity of baggage, guns, and ammunition to another train, and were soon on the way to our destination. A short run landed us at Blairgowrie, where an open carriage with four post-horses, ridden by smart, clever postilions in scarlet jackets, was in waiting, and we drove to the Queen's Hotel, where luncheon was provided. After a short halt we started for the Spital of Glen Shee, where amidst the Grampian Hills we were to follow our various sports. A heavy rain somewhat disconcerted us, but with such, to a sportsman, glorious ends in view what mattered a persistent downpour? The harder it rained, the sooner, we said, it would be over, and by the time we had traversed half the distance, the weather cleared, and we were able to admire the grand scenery of this wild portion of the Highlands of Scotland. Varied with wood and water, heather-clad hills, green meadows flushed with flowers of many hues, such as "the blue bells of Scotland," the wild ascabius, ox daisies, wild tares, interspersed with green broom, and here and there on barren spots tufts of heather just coming into bloom, crossing streams highly suggestive of large trout, we journeyed contentedly on, until the place was reached which was to be our headquarters for the season. A bright fire was burning, and we welcomed the warmth it afforded to us—the afternoon being both damp and cold. Our first business was to hear the report of the head-keeper, who informed us that grouse were plentiful, but strong on the wing and a trifle wild, but that in his opinion the good shots of the party might depend upon getting a bag of forty to fifty brace to each gun. "*Nous verrons,*" I mentally remarked; "I don't think I shall be in it if that is the number expected to qualify one to rank as 'a good shot;'" but "*nous verrons,*" and I looked entirely satisfied with the report, not leading that stalwart keeper to imagine for a moment that I had any doubts on the subject.

Next we inspected the kennel. The setters and pointers were all pronounced to be in high form. Then dinner was announced, and the loch trout that were served at once awoke a passionate desire in my breast to be amongst them. What matters it that the loch with an unspellable name, which I won't venture upon giving on so short an acquaintance, is seven miles distant? What are seven miles to an ardent disciple of Izaac Walton?—a mere nothing. What matters it that the hills are steep and the miles long?— Scotch miles are long, I am told. Of no consequence, I assure you, when such trout are to be caught. It is possible I may change my views on this head after I have tried, being somewhat like that "minstrel" we read of who found that the way was long and the wind was cold, he having become infirm and old; but I consoled myself by again observing, "*Nous verrons.*"

As I sit writing this a bright gleam of sunshine lights up the steep hillside, dotted all over with snow-white sheep, the clouds are rolling away, and a feeling of contentment passes through my mind, for there is promise of fair weather for the morrow, and to-morrow is the 12th of August, and we are to be up and on the Grampian Hills at 7 A.M.

CHAPTER II.

ON THE GRAMPIAN HILLS.

AFTER post-time on Thursday morning last, our small party of two guns strolled along the bank of the River Shee, on the chance of finding snipe and wild ducks, affording an opportunity, if we were fortunate enough to meet with any, of trying our guns, so that everything might be in order for a grand day's sport on the morrow. Arriving at a likely spot, the spaniel was not long in finding game. A wild duck being driven out of some sedgy grass, was instantly dropped by my skilful companion; and several snipe were found, but were too wide awake to let us get near them, and they sought safety in rapid flight. The banks of the Shee and the adjacent fields were literally carpeted with wild flowers of the brightest and most beautiful hues. Wild roses, bluebells, meadow-sweet, ragged robin, ox daisies (Marguerites), wild pansies, and other modest blooms offered facilities for making bouquets that could not be surpassed by the choicest flowers that all the skilled hands of the vendors in Covent-Garden could offer. Then, crossing a rickety bridge, we passed over the road and wandered along the hill-side. Soon a hare and rabbit were added to the list of the slain; then rose up a fine covey of strong grouse, which reluctantly we allowed to wing their way unmolested, for a time at any rate. Then we put up a large covey of partridges, and another snipe or two, and were satisfied that there was no lack of game on the estate of Rhidorach. After luncheon we drove along Glen Beg, which leads to Braemar and Balmoral, through the grandest scenery, the grim, rugged Grampian Hills towering gloomily over us; and the jingling of the bells on our high-couraged nag sounded cheerily as we wended our way to the keeper's house to make arrangements for the ensuing day. I was much struck with the beautiful reflection of the rainbows on the hillsides, several arcs of vivid brightness being visible on this occasion. To me it was a novel sight, though, from the frequent occurrence, the inhabitants of the glen were so accustomed to the sight that they paid little attention to this atmospherical display. Glen Beg is not always seen under such delightful auspices, as Alexander Robertson—the keeper—informed me that for fifteen weeks of the past winter the glen was impassable owing to the heavy fall and drifting of the snow; and he and the family, consisting of his wife and nine children, were cut off entirely from all communication with the outer world for this long period. When asked how he got on for food, he said he had laid up a large stock of oatmeal and dried fish, so that their wants were satisfied, having enough and to spare for some of his less fortunate neighbours. I should imagine they must have felt a trifle dull during that long and dreary winter time. All our arrangements being carefully made, we trotted back at a rattling rate to the Manse, to sleep—perchance to dream of a wondrous bag on the following day.

The morning of the 12th dawned brightly, giving promise of fine weather, though a strong nor'-wester was blowing, which would be against the shooter, if it continued.

Soon after six o'clock I was aroused by my cheerful host, and told that breakfast was ready, and that we were to start soon after seven. Thus far the programme was carried out to the letter, for we drove rapidly along the glen and reached our destination at eight o'clock, finding the keepers in readiness with the dogs, and a horse with panniers to carry our ammunition and luncheon, both being provided on a liberal scale, though not too liberal as regards cartridges, as was subsequently proved. Our party divided, each having a separate beat; whilst it was settled that I should accompany my host, a fine sportsman, a hale, hearty, muscular man, in the prime of life.

When the spot was pointed out on which we were to commence work I of course expressed my strong satisfaction; but a chill feeling came over me as I thought what a horrible failure my performance would be. That "rare place for grouse" up that rugged hill would, no doubt when reached, be all the keepers described it, but how was I to accomplish the feat? I am not in the prime of life—in fact, a good deal the other side. I grumble at having to mount the stairs in a tall house, and here I was to commence climbing one of the Grampian Hills in order to begin the day's work! I felt very much in the frame of mind that Mr. Winkle experienced when he was invited to try his hand at rook-shooting. I assumed the airs of a thoroughly competent workman—one who was accustomed to climb the steepest acclivities daily, as a matter of amusement—wishing all the time that I had candidly owned that I was unfit to play the part of a mountaineer even for one day only.

"Now then," said my companion, "let us be off;" and off we accordingly went, across the babbling burn which flows through the glen; and then my troubles commenced. Long before I had accomplished the half of my task I felt dead beat, I had hardly any breath left, and I thought it was all up with my day's shooting, so long and anxiously looked for. I said little—in fact I couldn't, I had no breath to give words to my feelings; and I silently resumed my toil, fortunately as it proved, for after a little while I found breath, the hill seemed less steep the higher I climbed, and when I reached the summit all signs of feebleness had passed away, my fear of turning out a fraud vanished, a sensation of complacency passed through me, and by a judicious concealment of my fears I had not damaged my reputation as a hardy, indomitable hill-climber.

Now, a black-and-tan Gordon setter steadily draws the patches of heather—in a few minutes he stands steady, then creeps on for a few paces, stands again, and up rises our first covey. Down drops this well-trained dog; bang! bang! go the guns; and our first brace is killed. Then on we go. In a second or two the setter has found more game, and another brace is bagged; and so we go on until ten o'clock, at which hour we had scored twenty-five brace. All sense of fatigue had by this time vanished, and I continued to walk through the heather, over the rugged stones, up hill, down hill, across the burns, and through spongy peat soil, resting at luncheon-time, and occasionally taking a seat on a boulder-stone, feeling as the day advanced that I was fresher than ever, and so continued until nearly eight o'clock, when a heavy shower came on, and we ceased shooting. So much for the fresh air of the Grampian Hills, which must be the sole cause of such a revival of strength; and strange to relate that, after walking, or, at any rate, being on my feet, for nearly twelve hours, I was as fresh as a four-year-old and "as fit as a fiddle."

As we mounted the heights we felt the full force of the wind, which was blowing half a gale; and as the grouse rose the strong breeze accelerated their pace, causing them to twist like snipe, which rendered it all the more difficult to bring them down. Still, on we went, every few minutes adding to our score, until the appointed place for luncheon was reached, by which time the bag was fifty brace. By the side of a small but swiftly-flowing burn we rested and refreshed. Never did cold beef taste so toothsome; never was there such a dish provided for hungry sportsmen as that ingeniously-designed and skilfully-executed compound of delicacies, worthy of Meg Merrilies, amongst which I traced the flavour of the timid hare, the wide-awake wild duck, the familiar rabbit, and the unappreciated moorhen, if I mistake not; whilst, tranquilly reposing in the cool waters of this humble stream, were several bottles, originally hailing from Rheims or Epernay. Just a wee drap of whuskey was handed to each of us, keepers, gillies, and a', and we were off again to increase our store. Nothing could exceed the beauty of the scenery. Meandering through the vale was seen the rippling stream, fed by many small accessories. trickling from the mossy sides of the adjoining hills; whilst the alteration in the lights and shades of these historic hills was something wonderful to note, varying, as they did, with the alternations of sunshine, gloomy clouds, and passing showers, which followed in rapid succession. Still, we were adding to our bag, notwithstanding the strong wind, my companion hitting eight out of every ten shots, the dogs working superbly, Robertson showing the utmost skill in their management and wonderful judgment in selecting the best places to find game, all of which would have been of little avail had not the shooter been well up to the work, for the ground is severe, and requires to be thoroughly well worked.

I have been accustomed all my life to participate, whenever I had a chance, in shooting game of all descriptions—the quail in the sugar plantations, the snipe, teal, widgeon, wild ducks in the low grounds, and the "bald pate" and the ground pigeon of the West Indies. I have seen battues of pheasants, drives of partridges, and all the various modes of capturing game, but I never saw sport equalling that of this day—at any rate, to my taste, for I love to witness the working of well-trained dogs, to see a long shot bring down a strong bird; and I care little for an enormous bag, though I like a good score which is won by hard work such as I joined in on this occasion, the grand total of two guns amounting to no less than a hundred and sixty-four head of grouse and one hare.

A rapid act of coachmanship resulted in a safe arrival at the Manse, where in due course we sat down to dinner, which proved not by any means the most unpleasant hour of the day. Proudly did our Piper, habited in full costume, not a riband, a feather, or any other of the gear of a true Highlander wanting, pour forth exciting war strains and Scottish tunes until one desired to fight somebody or something for the sake of Bonnie Scotland; no wonder that there are so many feats recorded in the history of Scotland when we think of the influence these martial strains of wild music had over the various spirited clans who fought and bled for their country.

Now that the undermining fear that I should break down whilst following these manly pursuits is dissipated, I contemplate with the utmost serenity the plans and prospects of the future. The ptarmigan are to be shot, and in order to find them the topmost ridges of these tall hills have to be surmounted; there, amidst the gray stones only, are they to be found; and if the day is warm and bright they may be readily approached. Time was—only a very few hours ago, in fact—when the idea of climbing those particular hills, pointed out as the home of the ptarmigan, would have caused me a twinge of intense regret when I contemplated the reality of the impending ascent and my inability to go up steep places. Now, as I contemplate my knickerbockers, the well-knit hose, and comfortable boots, I feel that I am to the manner born a Scotchman, and my mission, though hitherto unfulfilled, is to climb steep mountainsides in the pursuit of game. Then looming in the immediate distance is a first-class day in another glen, fixed for

Monday, where equally good sport with that on the 12th is expected; after which a day on Loch Na-Nean, which is situated at the head of Glentaitneach (or the pleasant glen), produces visions of delightful sport, the trout being abundant and fine. This loch, if I remember rightly, is the highest in altitude of all the Scotch lochs, and is distant from Glen Shee only some six or seven miles, a mere trifle for an athlete, consequently there will be no difficulty at all in traversing that distance.

Then, a little later, there is a deer-stalking to be enjoyed. A night in a hut in the forest, the early rising and pursuit of a "stag of ten," are things to be looked forward to; as also is the gathering and sports of the Highland Society, which takes place early in September. Trout fishing in the many modest little burns will not be neglected, for these fish, though small, are exceedingly sweet. *Probatum est*, for we had a dish for breakfast, provided by our esteemed and hospitable hostess, who with rod and line skilfully drew them out of a rippling rill in the vicinity of the Manse.

In considering the grand day's sport on the 12th, when the wind was blowing boisterously, I am greatly inclined to think that the many long shots which proved effectual were consequent upon the use of Schultze's cartridges, the powder burning freely, with a minimum of smoke, and evidently possessing great strength. This day (Saturday) was chosen as an easy walk over an indifferent line of country, the result of a short day's work being only twenty brace.

CHAPTER III.

CLIMBING THE CAIRNWALL.

FAMILIAR to those who have travelled from Blairgowrie to Braemar is the Cairnwall, one of the steepest and grandest of the Grampian Hills, exceeding 3000 feet in altitude, and standing boldly out amidst its companion heights in the lovely valley of Glen Beg. Around this noble hill, or, as it might more appropriately be styled, mountain, was the ground to which we journeyed at an early hour of the morning to shoot grouse, whilst enjoying the lovely scenery around us. Our party divided, one going with Ramsay, the second keeper, who had charge of the dogs; whilst I accompanied my friend, with Robertson, the head-keeper, and the other dogs, first having arranged a trysting-place where we were to meet at luncheon-time.

Scarcely had five minutes elapsed ere we commenced a day's sport which I have never seen equalled. Good as our first day proved, our bag on this occasion greatly exceeded it. When my companions first rented this moor, grouse were not plentiful; but with good management, a first-rate keeper, and fair shooting, the stock has greatly increased. The advantage to the proprietors of moors of having thorough sportsmen as tenants is obvious; whereas those who take the shootings simply for the slaughter of game, whose sole object is to be able to say that they have killed so many brace during the season, are in the end unprofitable customers. By killing the old birds the true sportsman ensures a better stock, whilst the pot-hunter who goes in for mere numbers does not kill the old cocks, except by chance, and slaughters the "cheepers," or young birds, remorselessly.

It would be useless for any other than a stout-framed muscular man, with a strong heart, to expect to shoot over such a moor as Rhidorach successfully. In order to get at his birds he must fearlessly climb the rugged mountainside, must not flinch from walking over the rolling stones hidden by the dense heather, or crossing the spongy morass, where, if he is not careful in avoiding the light green spots, he will probably find himself up to the hips in this treacherous ground, cooling his heels unwittingly in the hidden spring which trickles down the hillside, and swells the rushing stream of the burn that meanders through the beautiful valley. There can be no greater treat to a sportsman than to have the opportunity of witnessing the skilful working of dogs by a clever hand. For Highland shooting nothing can compare with the black-and-tan Gordon setters, for they are hardy, capable of standing any amount of work, and equal to living through the cruel cold winters of this latitude better than any other class of dogs.

The marvellous sagacity of these highly-trained animals is seen when Flora and Rap, two of this breed, are observed at work. At the wave of the keeper's hand, each dog instantly leaves his heels and quarters the ground backwards and forwards in search of the game; mind, with the wind full in their faces. Suddenly, as if by magic, Flora comes to a dead stand; this is the exact moment which unnerves the excitable or unpractised sportsman, for he knows he is in the immediate presence of the birds he is so eagerly pursuing. Steady stands Flora, with tail feathering and body quivering, whilst her bright intelligent eye is anxiously bent on the shooter to see if he is at hand ready to bring down the doomed grouse when he rises from his heather bed. Steadily is she backed up by Rap; then, whilst drawing closer and closer at a stealthy step, up rises the covey. Bang! bang! goes the breechloader; down drop a brace of birds right and left, and the well-broken dogs have "down-charged," as if instinctively, remaining immovable until the shooter reloads his gun. After a momentary pause the keeper waves his hand, motioning them to seek for the dead game, the sportsman steadily looking out for the "lazy bird" which remains *perdu* in the heather, whilst its companions have whirled away, winging their flight to some other favourite haunt on the wild hillside. Then up rises that lazy bird, but only to meet his doom. The dead game being picked up, the dogs are again at work. On this occasion my friend and companion opened the ball by killing ten birds out of eleven shots, fired within ten minutes. Shooting with a breechloader, having a choke-bore second barrel, he was able to make longer killing shots than I have ever seen accomplished before; and had it not been that he was thus provided and had an exceedingly straight eye, he would never have made such a bag, looking at the fact that owing to the cold, wet, windy season, the birds were unusually wild. For hour after hour we traversed the rough heather ground, covey after covey being put up, never rising without finding their numbers diminished, the sport being in the highest degree exciting and enjoyable. Looking down from on high on to the road which leads to Braemar, and on either side to which lies our shooting, I see our fellow-sportsman descending the hill, and we speedily meet at the Queen's Well, where the luncheon is unpacked, the wine placed in the cool stream that issues from the cavity in the rock, and rest and refreshment are the order of the day. Here we meet with Major Frank Tower—a fine shot at a rocketer, going as straight at a bird as he does across country—with his nephew, Mr. Egerton Tower, of the 95th Regiment, who bids fair to equal his uncle; both being guests of Mr. Christopher Tower, who rents the shooting adjoining Rhidorach, as far as Braemar. Talking of the morning's sport, Major Tower said that "grouse-shooting is the poetry of sport, and that to see dogs work, as good dogs do, is worth any expenditure of time and trouble to witness." When such an authority expresses so distinct an opinion, I feel I have not overstated my case when speaking of the first-class sport.

Renovated by rest and refreshment, I determined to quit the pleasant society of my friends for a while and to attempt the ascent of the Cairnwall. Having some knowledge of mountain-climbing, I steadily pursued my way, disturbing as I went covey after covey of grouse, the old cock-birds crying, as I thought, rather derisively, and in hoarse tones, "Caveck, Caveck, Caveck!" as they whirled away down the mountainside, and were speedily lost to view. Half the distance upwards being surmounted, I found myself amongst the gray old granite boulders amidst which the ptarmigan delight to dwell. Up rises a covey of six brace, wheeling about and disappearing round the hillside.

Resting for a minute or two I contemplated the summit which my ambition inclined me to surmount. This height, whilst appearing so near, yet proved to be far away, as I wended my steps upwards. The higher I rose the less trouble it was, and when I reached the summit, which, to be accurate in the highest degree, is a height of 3059 feet, I had not a symptom or feeling of fatigue. Sadly did I interfere with the quiet and comfort of the numerous coveys of ptarmigan who dwell amidst these granite stones, their plumage assimilating so closely to them that they are not discovered until they rise suddenly from their lurking-places and mount high in the air until lost to view in some more remote hiding-place.

From the very topmost ridge of Cairnwall, I look down upon the winding road along which crawls the four-horse coach which plies between Blairgowrie and Braemar, toiling to reach the Devil's Elbow, as sharp a turning as ever a vehicle of that description was called upon to twist round. Right down the glen the road to the Spital of Glen Shee is visible, a winding stream running between the rugged hillsides, dotted with countless sheep and lambs, which are merely so many white specks when seen at this height.

Looking around me, as far as the eye can reach I behold the vast range of the Grampian Hills.

Immediately opposite is the "Glas-Mille," a high, austere range of highland. Seen on a day such as that on which I viewed them—a day when sunshine and shade followed in rapid succession—I noted the various hues that the mountainsides assumed, dark brown now, light green next, sombre patches of blue-black, yellowish-green, and finally a "deeply, darkly, beautifully blue" tint were the prevailing colours that lighted up the landscape. Close at hand was the grim, gray, barren cairn, the Gaelic name of which I think I had better not attempt to give, but which being interpreted means the Aged Cairn—an expression that graphically describes this fine hill.

Far, far away I note amidst the cloud-clothed mountain-tops two or three patches of snow, distinctly visible even at the long distance. On one of the adjacent hills I observed two insignificant-looking lochs, which, however, have made their mark down the mountainside, wearing away the ground in their hasty passage towards the valley below, when swollen by the winter's snows and rapid thaws.

Having, as I sat upon a heap of stones, at the highest point on which was a dilapidated pole, which evidently at some time or other had been used as a flag-staff, deliberately surveyed the glorious prospect around me, I prepared to descend the steep side of Cairnwall, in order to join my companion. "*Facilis descensus averni,*" I think, was an observation made by some classic authority in one of the books which I was compelled unwillingly to study in the very far-off days of my youth. Doubtless that extremely downward journey to that place was easy enough, but my passage from the region above to the moorland below was not so light a task—the rough stones, the slippery moss, the frequent holes, rendering the descent far more difficult than the ascent; but by patient persistence, in a briefer space of time than I thought it would have taken me, I was at the base of the hill, which only two or three days back I looked upon as a height I could never expect to attain.

A wave of the hand from my jovial companion, who had just knocked down another brace, brought me to his side, and, leading me to a tranquil spot, bidding me rest on a moss-covered stone, he bade the attendant gillie bring forth from the rippling rill a bottle of the driest of dry champagne. "Rest, weary pilgrim, rest," said this friend in need, "and when we have drained the goblet to the dregs, we will be off and at them again." Accordingly we were off and at them again, with such success, as we toiled up the hills, through the heather, and over a specially rugged plateau of land—said to be the most favourite resort of the grouse—that it was necessary to despatch a horse with panniers to collect the heaps of birds deposited on the cairns or conspicuous stones on the "beats" we followed. It was not until the shades of evening closed around us that we ceased our sport, my companion having scored off his own gun no less a number than seventy-seven and a-half brace of grouse. This number was very largely augmented by our friend, who had worked the steepest corrie during this long day, and contributed not only grouse, but ptarmigan and hares as well. It is to me a surprising fact, after so long a walk and so steep a climb, that I felt no symptom of fatigue, and could have extended my walk if called upon to trudge home to the Manse, though not objecting, nevertheless, to mount the dog-cart, the jingling of the bells on the beautiful chestnut mare which conveyed us home sounding merrily as we rattled gaily along Glen Beg.

The weather, which had favoured us at first, now became variable, damaging the sport, for the grouse become wild and shy, and cock their heads up from the wet heather, and so are aware of the approach of their enemies. One day I started with Ramsay in full costume, with his pipes, to Kirkmichael, to witness the sports at the Strathardle Highland Gathering, held in the grounds of Dalnagar, Mr. James Small, of Dirnaneen, being the chieftain of the gathering. A large number were assembled, lining the side of the hill, which formed a natural amphitheatre, and most of the gentry resident in the neighbourhood, who desired to witness the favourite sports of tossing the caber, putting the heavy ball, throwing the hammer, reel-dancing, playing reels and strathspeys, etc. The weather somewhat spoiled the day's amusement, a miserable drizzle driving the ladies into the tent. Some of the Highlanders were marvellously fine specimens of athletes, displaying considerable grace in the dance and fleetness in the race.

Another day we drove to the Devil's Elbow, and on the steep hills which surround that picturesque spot we were to shoot grouse and ptarmigan. Killing my first shot, I started with good will to climb the tremendously tall hill before me. Steeper than ever was this climb, and I gladly availed myself of the offer of a considerate gillie to mount the sturdy horse that carried the panniers. How I was to accomplish this feat I was entirely ignorant. To mount a nag without stirrups or leathers on a steep hillside is certainly not easy of accomplishment, especially if the rider has passed the middle age and has a tendency to corpulence. " I'll just give you a leg up," said the gillie; and in a minute I found myself lying flat on the panniers, unable to get my legs over them, being seized with a fit of uncontrollable laughter at the absurdity of the position. At last this act of horsemanship was satisfactorily executed, and, laying hold of the horse's mane, I held on as he climbed slowly up the steep ascent. The weather continued stormy, and the total for the two guns was only twenty-one brace of grouse, one brace of ptarmigan, and two hares. The range of hills known as the Glasmiele, or "Stony Hill," is one of the highest points, and is exceedingly wild and grand, as, in fact, all the Grampians are. Returning to the keeper's lodge, we found strong tea, and an abundance of oatmeal cakes and scones, which, taken with delicious butter, formed a very acceptable meal on a wet, cold afternoon, especially after such a ride. Looking up to the top of a tall ridge, I saw an eagle hovering in the clouds, apparently ready to pounce down on some unfortunate animal. This bird would, the keeper informed me, probably measure seven feet six inches from tip to tip of its wings. Perhaps on some future occasion I may have a closer inspection of this now comparatively rare bird.

On Saturday we started for Ben Gouliping—I will not guarantee the spelling—but being interpreted it means "a hill behind a hill," and a remarkable tall climb it is to commence a day's sport with, and I think should be called Big Ben, for it is a teaser to mount to the summit. At length the spot is reached where business is to commence, and soon the grouse were falling to the shots of my skilful companions. The weather, however, turned exceedingly wet, spoiling the sport, and driving us home to shelter, the bag being only some twenty brace, and one brace ptarmigan. Not daunted by the heavy rain I persisted in climbing to the "Home of the Ptarmigan," and was rewarded by seeing some twenty brace on the wing, but only in the distance. Let us have a bright hot day, when they will lie close amidst the weather-beaten gray boulders, whose age it would be difficult to determine, then the keeper promises me that I shall kill some. Time will show, but as I killed two out of my three first shots, it is probable I may. To an elderly gentleman who has toiled up a steep hill, and then finds that the dogs are pointing in a still steeper place, and is called upon to mount quickly, though utterly out of breath, to that particular spot, it is rather a trial; but it has to be done, if you are to kill grouse on a Highland moor such as Rhidorach.

CHAPTER IV.

LOCH NA-NEAN.

THE wet weather necessitates a rest from the hard work which has been performed by the shooters on Rhidorach; affording an opportunity of making note of the wonderful sport that has been enjoyed and the varied pleasures experienced during a visit to the Highlands. The grandeur of the scenery when the sportsman is roving over the Grampians adds greatly to the pleasure of the sport; and he would be a soulless individual indeed who could, however intent on his sport, overlook and not feel excited by the glorious views that meet his eye as he mounts hill after hill in pursuit of the game. For my part, I cannot understand why so many people who talk glibly of the beauties of foreign lands have never visited Scotland. Each day during my stay has furnished some fresh delight; the wonderful change from the air of London to the invigorating breezes on the Grampian Hills enabling one to walk without fatigue, hour after hour, to places inaccessible to any other than pedestrians.

A day or two since the morning broke bright and clear, giving promise of a fine day, and it was decided that I should accompany my hostess in a climb, in order to have a look at Loch Na-Nean, described as "a very beautiful loch, situated at the head of Glentaitneach (or the Pleasant Glen). It is seven miles above the Spital of Glen Shee, is about a mile long by three-quarters of a mile broad, and is well stocked with splendid trout, said to be as fine as in any loch or river in Scotland, and weighing on an average three-quarters of a pound." To the other recommendations of Loch Na-Nean may be added the fact that it is the highest loch in Scotland, and that by the devious courses that have to be followed, the distance to the summit is increased to nine miles at least. Surely such a description as this was sufficient to create an ardent desire to prove the truth of the statement. At 9.30 A.M. we started, accompanied by George, the groom, a very smart active young fellow, charged with the care of our rods, lines, and also the very necessary luncheon-basket. My companion who was to take this long walk up so steep an incline was fitly habited for the work, wearing a light overcoat and strong but not too heavy yet well-nailed boots, the frequent heavy storms that occur in the Highland glens and mountain passes necessitating some such array as a protection against the sudden soaking showers that assail you, not without making their mark, and leaving you wet to the skin in a few minutes. I commend the overcoat of fine cloth to ladies intending to climb mountains or wander amongst these wild and rugged hillsides and romantic glens, suggesting that the dresses should be short, not reaching below the top of the boot in any case. Without the nailed boots the fair pedestrian would be, so to speak, nowhere—certainly not at the top of a Grampian Hill, amidst the gray stones in which dwell the ptarmigan. Add to these indispensable articles a stout walking-stick, and then, if the lady is young and active and accustomed to take regular exercise, she may venture on a tall climb. Failing these requisites, I should not recommend a trial, as in all probability it would result in a failure, and prove a mortification instead of a delight.

Away we went in the direction of the Pleasant Glen, and very pleasant we found it, though a trifle long, appearing, as mile after mile was trudged, as far from coming to an end as the life of a well-endowed annuitant, which anyone who has had the fortune to have the reversion knows, to his cost, to be greatly protracted. Contemplating in the distance the base of the high hill, to reach which I should have to walk at least eight miles, before climbing the last and steepest point—another mile or more—grave doubts passed through my mind as to the possibility of accomplishing the heavy task before me. I know that many great things have been accomplished by untiring patience, but in a matter of this sort—climbing a steep place—patience might be beaten on the post by a badly-fitting pair of boots, a faint heart, or a weak pair of legs. On we went through a group of stunted weather-beaten birch-trees, over some fairly even turf, following the course of the swiftly-flowing stream which owes its origin to the overflow of Loch Na-Nean.

Then we enter the Glen. The travelling now becomes more difficult. The ground is full of springs, and is of the order of the sponge spongy; the rough grass impedes you; small watercourses have to be crossed, tributary burns to be got over by aid of stepping-stones, on which, if tired, it is not always easy to preserve a balance, though the result of a slip is merely wet feet—unless you happen to fall prone into the rippling stream by-the-bye. All this while we are gradually ascending towards the summit of our desires: now magnificent weird mountains look down upon us on either side; there is a beautiful waterfall, contributing to the ever-babbling stream; the music of the water, the bleating of the sheep, and the barking of the collies being the only sounds that we hear. Then my companion calls attention to a golden eagle high soaring in the air, casting anything but a "sheep's-eye" on the lambs below, doubtless selecting one particular victim to swoop down upon and bear away to his home on the top of yon stony, steep, and hoary hill. At that moment up rises the ever-watchful shepherd, and the wary eagle mounts higher and higher, and sails majestically over a neighbouring mountain, and is lost to sight. I am glad to hear that Colonel Farquharson of Invercauld, the laird of this wild domain, instructs his keepers on no account to shoot these grand birds, already far too rare.

By midday we had traversed a considerable portion of the glen, and thought, ere beginning to climb the rugged, steep ascent, that it would be as well to take luncheon, in order to fortify ourselves for the labour before us. Resting for half an hour, we refreshed ourselves with the water of the stream by the side of which we reclined (in my case qualifying the water with just a dash of whisky).

Then began the real hard work of the day: keeping along the course of the stream, crossing ever and again over the stepping-stones in order to avail ourselves of the slightest advantage of a level spot that presented itself; then along a narrow sheep-track, the water all the while noisily leaping from ledge to ledge, in haste to join a stream springing from a hill in Glentaitneach, and another from Glen Beg, which, when united, form the Shee. This meeting of the waters is the meaning of the Gaelic word "spital."

Still higher and higher as we ascend, steeper and steeper it becomes. I fancy we must have nearly reached the summit, but a ridge only has been surmounted. There, far away, is the end of our climb, and many a difficult and slippery path will have to be followed ere we reach the loch. It was toil, but pleasant toil, and by slow degrees we were accomplishing our work, my companion climbing bravely, undaunted by difficulties and regardless of danger, as she crossed and recrossed the stream by means of the slippery boulders which formed the stepping-stones, without a slip or false step. The end is at last in view, near at hand, but difficult to climb, being the steepest bit of the whole. But in a quarter of an hour we had gained the top, and were gazing on Loch Na-Nean in all its beauty on this bright clear pleasant day; then, throwing myself down upon the heather, I exclaimed, somewhat after that Peri who is described by the poet as having attained Paradise: "Joy, joy for ever; the task is done. The mountain's climbed the loch is won."

After a few minutes' rest the gillie who was in attendance launched the boat, and we prepared to fish as we floated over the too tranquil waters of the loch

—a ripple being necessary for successful angling. However, a brief space only elapsed ere my fair companion hooked a fish, and by the aid of her landing-net secured one of nearly a pound weight, the most beautiful specimen of the pink trout I have ever seen, spotted all over, and when just out of the water showing the most brilliant colours of divers hues.

Our attention then is attracted to a double shot, which echoed over the hills, and we see our friend at the top of one of the steep eminences which surround us. He is well among the ptarmigan, and we note that the covey escapes, but in diminished numbers, for a brace has fallen to his well-directed shot. The difficulty of shooting over such a beat as my friends had chosen, covering as it did the hillsides of Glentaitneach and the hills above the loch, must be seen to be appreciated. Even after the performances I have witnessed, I was astonished to see the work they performed, bagging over forty brace even on such trying ground.

Still we continued to float tranquilly on the bosom of this exalted loch, catching more of the finny tribe, and rendering the weight of our basket heavier for the downward than it was for the upward journey.

Grand in the extreme is the view from Loch Na-Nean, as you look upon the Grampian Hills and the extensive deer forests of Attonaur, the property of the Earl of Fife, on the one hand; and Fealar, belonging to the Duke of Athole, on the other. It is upon the two bright green islands in the middle of the loch that innumerable gulls resort to lay their eggs and rear their young. A transformation scene of an unusual character is then to be noted, the ground being perfectly white with myriads of gulls, who on rising change the view to the natural vivid green which characterises these islands.

At 5.30 we commenced our descent, which, though difficult, was more readily accomplished than our upward climb. Care, however, was necessary in getting down the first mile, every step having to be chosen with caution, as a trip would have brought one to grief, the grass being very slippery in places. By degrees we reached a less precipitous part of the descent, and our rate of progress increased. Then we were joined by our friend, whose gillie was well laden with ptarmigan, and together we marched along the seemingly never-ending glen. On we went, following and crossing the swift-flowing stream with unflagging exertion, but still the end of the Pleasant Valley seemed as far off as ever. Presently we met a lady, one of our pleasant party, who could not be persuaded to join us in our climb; for, being devoted to art, she would not lose the opportunity of putting the finishing-touches to a painting of one of the lovely views in the vicinity of the Manse.

Still we trudged on as we had done for the last two hours and a half, until at length we reached the sheeppen which we had observed on our upward journey. Then we crossed the bridge, and marched through the clump of stunted birches. "Now," said our companion —he who, red-handed with the blood of ptarmigan, was for the time our guide—" we have only three miles and a half to accomplish our journey." Well, what are three miles and a half when you have been on your legs all day? The sturdy pedestrian in the heyday of life will answer, "A mere nothing;" but let him live to attain to the age I am unwillingly compelled to acknowledge, and he will find, if he reaches that late period of life, that the miles are *fur-longer* than were those of our youth.

Patience, however, had borne me up the steep acclivity, and surely it would not fail me now; so, assuming a jaunty air, I affected a total unconcern as to the distance yet to be traversed ere the long day's work could be completed. Bravely my companion stepped out as we neared our haven of rest and repose; then, ascending a slight rise that leads to the Manse, we entered gaily, showing but slight signs of fatigue; and, as I looked upon my light-hearted and agreeable companion, I mentally repeated the words of Scott:

> A foot more light, a step more true,
> Ne'er from the heath-flower dashed the dew;
> E'en the slight harebell lifts its head
> Elastic from her airy tread.

CHAPTER V.

AMONGST THE PTARMIGAN.

THE bells on the chestnut mare tinkle merrily as we journey at a rattling pace to Rhidorach, performing the distance of three miles in a very brief space of time. "The native hue of resolution" in my case is very far from being "sicklied o'er with the pale cast of thought"—very much the contrary, in fact. Far, far away, somewhere down in the Lowlands, I left dull care behind me; and my thoughts are of the pleasantest description, as befits one who is in the enjoyment of all the luxuries and comforts of life. But, as regards resolution, mine is fixed; I am determined to ascend the stony heights of the grim old mountains in the hope of getting a few shots at the ptarmigan, though I am warned that after so much wind and rain they are certain to be very wild. However, if I merely have a glimpse of some of these beautiful birds I shall be quite satisfied and well rewarded for the trouble, or rather I should say the pleasure, of a climb amidst such grand and, to-day, glowing scenery; for the sun, by way of a change, is shining brightly over hill and dale, moorland and mountain. Alighting at the keeper's lodge, I laid hold of the double-barrelled breechloader, and filling my pockets with cartridges, started for Cairn Moor, in order to reach which it was necessary to climb a steep ascent of about a mile. My first business was to cross the burn, swollen with the heavy rain of the previous day; but it was no easy matter to jump from stepping-stone to boulder. I had no stick to aid me, and, weighted with cartridges and gun in hand, I found it a difficult matter to preserve an even balance. But all such obstacles were surmounted; and on I toiled, catching hold of the heather to aid me in mounting the steep bit which I had first to encounter. When I had gained the height before me I sat down breathless, the perspiration dropping in large beads from my forehead. After a few minutes' rest and a long pull and a strong pull at the flask of "whuskey," I started again, gradually recovering from the state of breathlessness as I mounted higher and higher. Then, at my very feet, up rises "a lazy bird," which went on its way rejoicing, as I had not put cartridges in the breechloader; for, until I got my second wind and was a little firmer on my legs, I thought it unadvisable to load, as walking with both barrels at full cock over the rugged moorland is not a particularly safe proceeding. By degrees the difficulty experienced at first vanished, and I gained the summit without fatigue, being rewarded with a magnificent view of the "sma' hulls and muckle hulls" around me. There were the solemn old mountains, the Glas Muol, the Cairnwall, the Aged Cairn (looking less grim than usual, for the sun shone brightly, bringing out the colour vividly); there a patch of purple heather, here a piece of bright green grass, and towering above all are the gray heads of these venerable hills; whilst through the correi or valley runs the brawling burn, sparkling in the sunlight as it leaps from ledge to ledge. Now a mountain hare steals slyly away, but quite out of reach. Then I traverse the bed of old gray boulders, amongst which the ptarmigan are found; up rises a covey of six brace, mounting high in the air and wheeling away—never within shot. Then a second lot takes wing before I get within three hundred yards of them; next comes another hare on foot which gives me a wide berth. At length I have a long shot at a single bird, which, however, escapes scot free. All this was rather disheartening; but, at any rate, I was clearly amongst the ptarmigan. My companion, however, who was on a lower level, was more successful, bagging a brace in addition to a lot of grouse. One of the charms of this part of Scotland is the varied nature of the game you meet with. Looking at the place where the game hangs I noticed grouse, ptarmigan, snipe, wild duck, hare, rabbit, venison, and trout from the loch, with lesser ones from the burn; golden plovers are also met with occasionally. Rabbits are very numerous in places, choosing positions, however, difficult for the sportsman to reach. The hares at present are " merry brown hares," but will soon be changing to their winter colour—white. By the time I reached the place agreed upon for that pleasant and much-needed refection, luncheon, the weather had become exceedingly cold, unusually so for the month of August. The ice had been as thick as a shilling in the early morn, and it seems that at some period of every month since October last there has been frost. The crops are quite green, and I should imagine that very little, if any, corn will be harvested in the Highlands this year. The sheep-farmers, however, seem to be doing well. One holding an extensive run on Rhidorach has some six or seven thousand, and large numbers are found travelling to the different markets, blocking up the narrow Highland by roads so as to render it occasionally a work of time and patience to drive through the large flocks that go bleating along. Then is the time to note the marvellous sagacity of the shepherd's dog, and the skilful way in which he disperses the sheep and afterwards collects them together when you have passed through. *Mais, revenons à nos moutons,* or rather to our particular cold mutton, which was the "diet" provided for the occasion: this was quickly disposed of. I am now reminded of an anecdote I heard the other day *à propos* of meals. A Scotch gentleman found himself seated at dinner by the side of an extremely voluble young lady, whose flow of chatter wearied him so that he dryly remarked: "Hoot, lassie; we're met for meat and no for clavers." Well, I think that gentleman was right; there is a time for everything. Having met with so little success with the ptarmigan, by the advice of Ramsay, the keeper, I abandoned the intention of having another climb in pursuit of this very wild game, descending to a lower level and witnessing the admirable behaviour of Lorne, who found and stood to the game with wonderful steadiness. Soon my companion floored a brace; one, a cunning old cock-bird, being merely winged, contrived to find refuge in a deep hole, which caused Ramsay much trouble before he drew him from his hiding-place. Then Lorne finds again. This time he stands so steadily that we are certain birds are close to him; but I was not prepared to see one right under his nose

—a young bird, lying so close in the heather that it could hardly be induced to rise. I saw on another occasion a young bird taken by the keeper by hand, and perfectly uninjured. It now became evident that the time for making big bags of grouse was over. The gusty weather and continued wet had caused them to pack. One lot, estimated at a hundred brace, and another of half the quantity, rose wildly on our appearance on a very rough piece of moorland, rising high in the air, going over the hills and far away in no time. Once these birds are gathered together in packs, you may depend upon having to work hard indeed to make a decent bag; the total this day falling to two guns being only eighteen brace of grouse and two brace of ptarmigan.

Another day, the birds being so extremely wild, we started for Rhidorach with the intention of having "a grouse drive." This was accomplished by the aid of five gillies and myself, determined to try how I could perform as a beater. My friends having proceeded to the favourite correi, through which the grouse were to be driven, laid down in the heather, and concealed themselves as much as they could, while we stalked over the moor and hill-tops, starting the coveys which betook themselves to the pass where the shooters were in ambush. In my anxiety to accomplish my task in a satisfactory manner, I was afterwards told I took an unnecessary amount of trouble; toiling along the side of a precipitous hill, over the treacherous boulders, passing whenever possible along the extremely narrow sheep-track; ever and anon startling the grouse from their heather beds, and causing them to fly in the direction where the two shooters were ready to bring down any that came within their reach. For nearly three hours I continued the promenade. The result of the drive was small, eight and a-half brace only being brought down; but then it must be remembered that the grouse flew at a very great height and extreme pace, and that only those accustomed to bringing down rocketers had any chance at all. To me, save for the purpose of swelling the total of the slain, the sport was poor. I missed the treat of seeing the dogs work; and they missed the sport also, for when we passed the kennel and left them behind a continuous howl was raised on their finding they were not to accompany us. So clever are these well-trained dogs and so fond of the work, that they immediately burst into a wild and long-protracted chorus when they hear the jingling of the bells on that fleet steed that draws their masters to the keeper's lodge. The weather continued unsettled, and the birds were very wild. Soon after luncheon a Scotch mist enveloped the hill-tops, and a heavy rain fell in the correi, drenching me to the skin in a few minutes. One of the perils of the moors is this dense mist which suddenly spreads over them, and in which the sportsman may readily lose himself, and have to pass the night on the hills or in the correis, should he not be clever at finding his way. The only safe course in such mishap is to find, if you can, a rippling burn, and then to follow its downward course. But this is not an easy or pleasant way of spending even a portion of the night.

One day we shoot on another favourite ground, to arrive at which it is necessary to climb for an exceedingly long time. The entire morning's shooting has to be performed on rising ground. A wide expanse of moorland is before you, and grouse are abundant, but the climb is a stiff one, and requires an amount of toil that would dishearten ordinary shooters. Let only that wild hillside be reached, and then, if you hold your gun straight, all your trouble will be compensated for by the number of grouse that will fall to your gun. Bang! bang! goes the breechloader, and I see that the shooter has made his mark, for an old bird, being heavily hit, "towers," flying straight upwards as long as life lasts, then twisting and tumbling it falls from its high altitude, dropping dead at my feet. A bird of beautiful plumage and fine condition was this, probably three or four years old, its legs being closely feathered down to the extremity.

As we journeyed along I came upon a little rill with a tiny waterfall, by the side of which was a lovely bed of ferns, growing luxuriantly around the basin; the purple heather blooming beautifully in this sheltered nook.

Owing to the heavy rainfall, this part of the moor was so wet that it was only to be compared to a moist sponge on a large scale, and the walking was most difficult. Forgetting for a moment the caution I had received when I first entered on the moor as to treading on the very light green mossy spots that are so frequently met with, I set my foot on what appeared to be safe ground, but only to find myself up to the knees in the cold spring and deep mud of this man-trap. Very cold was that water when it trickled over the tops of my boots, admonishing me to use more caution for the future when traversing a mossy piece of moorland.

After luncheon the rain came on in heavy showers, and the heather became so wet that birds would not lie, even if it cleared, and nothing remained to be done but to wend our way homewards.

As I sit writing in the Manse, the sun shining brightly, I cannot but note the beauty of the scene. Prior to the occupation of this comfortable abode by the newly-ordained minister, my friends were fortunate enough to secure it for a few weeks from the incoming tenant, a gentleman of culture and refinement, as shown by his well-stored library of choice books—of inestimable value, if only as a means of killing time in such winters as the last, when the road was blocked by snow for many weeks. Seen under those circumstances, the prospect from the window I am now sitting at must have been widely different from the smiling aspect the place now assumes. Placed in a sheltered spot, a steep bit of hill being immediately at the back, and facing a south aspect, a long view is obtained of the valley, the high hills, and the swift-flowing Shee. At this period of the year the oats in front of the Manse are perfectly green, showing no signs of coming into ear at present. Haymaking is progressing in a highly dilettante style. Up the snow-white walls of the minister's house a tropæolum of a delicate carmine hue climbs; several rose-trees are in full, profuse bloom, one being of a specially beautiful description; a laburnum is also to be seen in full blossom; whilst green gooseberries and currants are to be gathered in the garden. This contrasts greatly with what we experience in England, where most of the foregoing flowers and fruits are long since over.

CHAPTER VI.

FAREWELL TO THE HIGHLANDS.

"Come what come may, Time and the hour runs through the roughest day," Shakespeare tells us, and my experience proves it true also of the fairest and pleasantest periods of our enjoyment; for the time has now arrived when I must bid farewell to the Highlands, and the varied sports enjoyed in that favoured part of Scotland.

The day prior to our departure was fine, though a stiff breeze was blowing, which, as we climbed the hills, made itself felt, and caused the birds to rise at very long distances, rendering it difficult for shooters to make a good bag. Not being satisfied with the result of my sport amongst the ptarmigan, I determined to make a supreme effort on the last day that I should have the opportunity of adding to my score. I chanced to read a few days since some facts in natural history, showing that the "upper limit of the common grouse is 1800 feet; the range of the white grouse or ptarmigan extending from 1800 to 3000 feet."

A wonderful provision of nature was pointed out by the head-keeper, who showed me a feather of the ptarmigan, within which was a second small feather of soft down, forming a lining, which affords extra protection from cold for the birds abiding on the higher range of the hills; whilst the common grouse, which lives at a lower level, has no such provision made.

It was on the mountain-tops that I was to go on this occasion to enjoy the exciting sport of shooting ptarmigan. In order to do this I had to walk some two miles or more over the rough, rising, and in places boggy ground, before the base of the mountain was reached, up which I had to climb in order to get within shot of these wary birds. It was no easy task to attain the topmost ridge. However, following the under-keeper, I, after considerable exertion, surmounted the difficulty, and stood on the summit, breechloader in hand. In order to find the ptarmigan, it was necessary to struggle over the immense beds of loose granite stones which covered the mountainside, seeming as if at some time, ages ago, there had been an eruption of granite stones, so thickly did they lie down the hillside. Balancing myself as well as I could, holding my gun as carefully as possible, both barrels being at full cock, I stepped upon these treacherous stones, which frequently gave way under my feet, rolling down the steep declivity.

Up rises the first covey, but not within reach of my gun: we mark them down, one alighting on a ledge, up to which I was bound to climb if I intended to have a shot. With tottering steps, and almost breathless, I reached the spot, and Ramsay pointed out a ptarmigan sitting amongst the stones, which, from the similarity of its plumage to the gray and moss-spotted boulders, was difficult to discern. For many minutes I looked in vain for the bird, though it was within twenty yards of me; but at length I espied it. I had a fair chance as it took wing, but missed it, and the ptarmigan, rising high in the air, vanished from my gaze. It was the last twenty yards of that tall climb that incapacitated me from taking good aim. I could with difficulty keep my balance; I had to take care that I did not shoot the keeper, or my friend and the gillies, whom we met at this point. No wonder that I missed the bird; the wonder was that I was there to miss it, for it was the roughest walk I ever took in pursuit of any game.

Then we rested for a few minutes beside one of the countless bright, clear, cold springs that trickled down the mountainsides, and refreshed ourselves with the pure water, necessarily qualified with whisky. Then we resumed our sport, and my companion, stout of limb and full of vigour, soon was amongst the ptarmigan, adding largely to the bag; though the birds were wild and could only be got at when scattered and rising singly. After my friend I toiled, with difficulty holding my own, until the trysting-place was reached and the luncheon-basket opened. Having had half-an-hour's rest we started again, my companion suggesting that I should climb another mountain, higher than any I had yet ascended, in order to see the view, as well as to follow the ptarmigan, which he had marked down on its height. Accompanied by Ramsay, I wended my way up Cairn Yourn, being well rewarded for the trouble of mounting its steep side by the view of the grand scenery around it.

As far as the eye could reach were tall mountains, lochs glistening in the sunshine, valleys through which meandered bright sparkling streams; which at this distance resembled fine threads of silver as you traced their course through the distant correis far away. The atmosphere this day being clearer and brighter than on any other during my visit, I see the Lomonds, a tall range of mountains towering towards the sky Varied and beautiful indeed is the prospect, the light and shade alternating, and the whole forming a panorama of wild scenery as grand as any I have ever seen. Looking on the other side, I see the hills in the vicinity of Braemar, the tall summits being enveloped in gloomy clouds, sombre and grand, a contrast to the blooming picture I had just turned from. As I resume my walk up rise thirty brace, then a covey of six brace. We get single shots and scatter a covey, marking some down on the side of a far-off hill. After a brisk walk the place is reached. Lorne, our handsome black-and-tan setter, points, standing as firm as a rock. Up rises a ptarmigan, only to fall dead amongst the heather. The rest of the covey rise, and are off to a more secure resting-place, but I mark and follow them again with success, until the time arrives to make for the keeper's lodge, where I was to join my companion. Arriving there I found him awaiting me, and so ended the last and not least exciting of our many days' fine sport, the total bag being thirteen brace of grouse and fourteen and a-half of ptarmigan, as well as several hares. Whilst resting during this hard day's work, Ramsay pointed out the spot where, in a cave, lie buried the bodies of those slain in a fray between the men of Glen Isla and the men of Glen Shee, in the bow-and-arrow time, as he termed it—rather an indefinite, but certainly a distant, date. In those days the Spital of Glen Shee, Glen Thaitneach, and Glen Beg had numerous inhabitants, as shown by the ruins of many houses, then occupied by small crofters, who owned sheep and cattle, which fed on the adjoining hills and moors. Now the only houses in that district can be counted on the fingers of two hands. A feud existed between the men of these glens, caused by a habit of cattle-raising, the Highland caterans having a rooted idea that it was their mission to steal other people's cattle, which naturally led to complications, and finally to a battle on what is now the highroad to Braemar. On one side were ranged the men of Glen Isla, and on the other slope the men of Glen Shee, led by a noted chief, Cam-rhoua by name—otherwise the red man—a diminutive and deformed being, but possessed of much courage and cunning, and a notable marksman, whose arrow seldom missed its aim. As a specimen of his craft and quickness of perception a tale is extant that on one occasion several caterans came in search of him, seeking his life in retaliation for some kinsman slain in one of the neighbourly raids that were common in those parts. Noting their approach, he at once assumed the ways and appearance of a daft cheild, which thoroughly deceived the visitors who had so unceremoniously entered his home; then, taking up their bows one by one, he shot the arrows as far as possible. Still not suspecting that he was the man they were in search of, they told him, as he had fired the arrows away, he must go and pick them up. This he did; and, having thus gained a good start, he escaped without difficulty from his enemies. But to resume the account of the battle: The men being drawn up within four hundred yards of each other, the fight began; the caterans and men of Glen Isla, making true aim, the men of Glen Shee fell fast, and showed a disposition to retreat. All this while, Cam-rhoua was lying in a secluded spot, having made a vow not to engage in the strife until the sun had passed over him; but, on hearing that the men of Glen Shee were falling fast and needed support, he caused himself to be carried to a cave over which the sun shone sooner than on his late resting-place. Then calling to the captain of the caterans, "man for man," he advanced, and laid him low with his first arrow, shooting all the pick of the enemy, and finally gaining a grand victory for the men of Glen Shee. The bodies of sixty caterans were borne away, and others remained unclaimed, the dead of the victorious side being buried where they fell, in the cave which was pointed out to me, and which may be readily seen by those travelling between the Spital and Braemar; the site being close to the "Queen's Well." Such was the story I listened to, as I rested on a piece of rough rock.

> I cannot tell how the truth may be,
> I tell the tale as 'twas told to me.

Before concluding it may be as well to give a few words of information to those unacquainted with the Highlands of Scotland and the way in which sport is to be obtained. The price of a moor commences at the diminutive figure of 5*l.*; whilst the cost of a deer forest reaches to the large rental of 7000*l.* per annum.

This, of course, is an entirely outside price; and many good deer forests, with plenty of grouse shooting, are obtainable for sums of 1000*l*. or 2000*l*. A deer forest being pointed out to me, I naturally alluded to the total absence of trees—not a single one was visible; a forest being but a mountain side or pass, the favourite resort and abiding-place of deer, which are jealously preserved. The shootings on level moors command high prices, as it is easy work to make a big bag when the grouse are driven by a host of beaters to you. On a moor like Rhidorach a man must be able to endure any amount of fatigue and to earn every bird by " the sweat of his brow." Of deer-stalking there are two courses by which an antlered head is to be secured. The first is by renting an expensive and well-stocked deer forest, and having a drive, the shooter being placed at convenient spots by which the deer pass, slaughtering the animals without trouble or exertion. The other mode is to stalk the stag over moor and mountain, being on the ground before daylight, often following in pursuit for a whole day without obtaining a shot, taking long detours to get the wind of the stag, crawling then a mile or two on hands and knees, through the burns, over the boulders noiselessly; lying down at times to avoid detection, at length creeping stealthily until within range, and then, if your hand is steady and you are cool and unexcited, you may occasionally bring down a stag with each barrel. Of the Highlanders I must say I formed a most favourable opinion. They are shrewd, civil, and obliging, without showing a sign of servility. Well-informed, as a rule, steady, domesticated, and thorough lovers of sport; warming to a congenial spirit, and making themselves pleasant and agreeable. Amongst the shepherds I met with men thoroughly acquainted with the topics of the day. Living amongst the mountains he has plenty of time for reading whilst tending his large flock. Contented with his lot, which appears to be a little dull—

> No thoughts hath he but thoughts that pass
> Light as the wind along the grass.

Of the keepers too high praise cannot be given; thorough sportsmen, first-rate breakers and managers of dogs, well acquainted with the habits of every description of game and their haunts and favourite spots during different periods of the year, it is in their power to aid the shooter greatly in making a good bag, more especially if they find they are working with a true sportsman, who appreciates their exertions.

After wishing a cordial good-bye to those dwelling in the Spital of Glen Shee and the immediate vicinity, we posted at a rapid rate to Blairgowrie, thence by train to Perth, where we received every possible attention; our luggage was carefully disposed of, not a package being found wanting, though their name was legion. Shown into a similar carriage to that in which we travelled when going north, we in due course went to bed, to find on awaking that we were within twenty miles of London. Our party broke up on arrival at Euston, mutually pleased with the sport and society we had enjoyed, and regretting the necessity of drawing our visit to a close, and bidding farewell to the Highlands for awhile.

CHAPTER VII.

THE BRAEMAR GATHERING.

> Breathes there a man, with soul so dead,
> Who never to himself hath said,
>   This is my own, my native land!
> Whose heart hath ne'er within him burned,
> As home his footsteps he hath turned
>   From wandering on a foreign strand.
> If such there breathe, go, mark him well;
> For him no minstrel raptures swell;
> High though his titles, proud his name,
> Boundless his wealth as wish can claim;
> Despite those titles, power, and pelf,
> The wretch, concentered all in self,
> Living shall forfeit fair renown,
> And doubly dying, shall go down
> To the vile dust, from which he sprung,
> Unwept, unhonoured, and unsung.
> *Lay of the Last Minstrel.*

IF you would see pride of nationality displayed, historic traditions observed, and old feelings of clanship maintained, then attend the annual gathering at the Castletown of Braemar; and note well the bearing of the braw Hielanders, retainers of the Laird of Invercauld and the Earl of Fife, when they march on the ground with banners flying to the martial music of the bagpipes, in order to take part in the athletic games and many sports, which are so heartily entered into and contested with so much spirit and good-tempered rivalry, by the sturdy clansmen who assemble in considerable numbers on the occasion of this popular gathering.

Braemar being within a comparatively short distance of Balmoral, the proceedings have often been honoured by the presence of Her Majesty; a fact that adds largely to the excitement of the scene, and calls forth the most strenuous exertions on the part of the competitors to bear off the honours of the day. It was an exceedingly bright morning in the early part of September last (1881), when I started for the Spital of Glen Shee, to drive a distance of fifteen miles to attend these Highland pastimes; but notwithstanding "the merry, merry sunshine," the cold was severe, a sharp wind blowing over the wild country, giving a foretaste of winter and a hint of the sort of weather to be expected now that the autumn was on the wane. My companions were two stalwart Highlanders, who were going to join the men of Invercauld, habited in full costume, and representing good specimens of the clan to which they belonged. After journeying some three miles we stopped for a few minutes at the keeper's lodge. At that time of the year a residence in so retired a locality may be all very well; but when Glen Beg is blocked up with snowdrifts and the roads are impassable for many weeks at a time, I can readily believe in the loneliness of the inhabitants. However, Robertson and his wife, with the companionship of ten children of all ages, manage to weather the storms and tempests of the winter season, and seem thoroughly contented with their lot in life.

The Highland passes are greatly afflicted with the presence of professional tramps—sturdy ill-looking villains, who wander over the country, begging from door to door, and exacting alms often by threats or through the fears of the inhabitants of these lonely spots. One instance was given by Mrs. Robertson of the audacity of one of the ruffians, who, during the absence of her husband, sought to obtain relief. Not liking the appearance of the tramp, she attempted to close the door upon him; but he forced his way into the house, and, straightway went up to the table where the children were eating their dinner, and, taking a spoon from the hand of one of the little ones, helped himself, *sans cérémonie*, to the porridge.

"Eh, sir," said Mrs. Robertson, "but I could na' stand that, so I took down my husband's gun from its place on the wall and presented it at his head. Then, dashing down the spoon on to the floor, he opened the door and was off at full speed down the glen. Eh, perhaps he would na' have run quite so fast had he had an inkling that the gun was not loaded."

Then, proceeding on our way, we ascended the steep hills, winding round the Devil's Elbow, until we reached the highest point in the road, some 2500 feet above sea-level. After this we travelled along at good speed, it being down-hill nearly all the rest of the journey, noting as we passed along the Cluny Water, a swift-flowing river, that at proper seasons holds abundance of salmon, joining the Dee in the vicinity of Braemar. Then we approach Callater, passing Tolmount, a rugged mountain or "muckle hull," as the inhabitants would describe it, of an elevation of 3143 feet, and other grim mountains of about the same height; away by the lodge in the occupation of Mr. Christopher J. H. Tower, who has the Callater shooting and deer forest. Then soon Braemar is reached, and we put up at the Invercauld Arms, a noted hotel, greatly frequented by tourists who visit this part of the Highlands. By this time I was chilled to the bone, and gladly availed myself of the opportunity of partaking of some real Scotch broth, in order to counteract the effects of the long cold drive of three hours.

A charming and prosperous place is Braemar, studded with comfortable residences; the River Dee tumbling and dashing along its rocky course, crossing which you come to another grand hotel, The Fife Arms, which also enjoys a large amount of patronage. By this time the hour was near at hand when the sports were to commence, and I made my way to the appointed place and found a number of persons assembled in the vicinity of the ruins of the castle, which are, to some extent, restored and fitted up for the occasion, one room being prepared for the ball which was to be a suitable conclusion to this festive gathering. I then learnt that, to the great disappointment of all present, the Queen would not attend the sports on this occasion; a fact which was due in all probability to the extreme coldness of the weather. Another cause of regret was the absence of Colonel Farquharson, who was called away by the severe illness of his brother; the duty of directing the sports and entertaining the numerous visitors falling upon Mr. Foggo, the factor of the Invercauld estates, who most assiduously and pleasantly performed the rôle of master of the ceremonies, discharging to the satisfaction of all present the duties which devolved upon him in the absence of the laird.

First to appear upon the scene were the men of Invercauld, who, headed by their pipers, all being in full costume, marched proudly on to the ground, and took up their position, ready to give a cordial reception to the Earl of Fife and his Highlanders, who followed quickly, preceded by no less than five pipers. Cordial was the greeting given to them, and loud and long continued the cheers as they drew up opposite to the retainers of Colonel Farquharson: the scene at this time was exciting in the extreme, and one could not fail but to be pleased with the appearance of the fine body of men assembled to compete for the prizes and honours of the meeting in amicable rivalry. With little loss of time the sports commenced, and prodigious were the feats of strength and skill that were performed in throwing the heavy hammer, putting the stone, tossing the caber. Then followed what was to me the most pleasing part of the day's festivity, the spirited dancing of these agile men in the four-handed reels, which were executed most cleverly, and at the same time gracefully and with great spirit; and to ordinary observers it was not easy to decide who was entitled to the palm of victory, so excellent were the competitors in the arduous and difficult trial of skill and endurance. Judging from the applause which followed, it would appear to be a most popular pastime. À propos to the appearance of the Highlanders when habited in full costume, an amusing anecdote is told of the late keeper on Rhidorach, who on the occasion, some years since, of a visit that was paid by the Queen to the Laird of Invercauld, in reply to a question put to him by Her Majesty, asking how it was that the peasantry in the Highlands were so much better clothed than those in any other part of her dominions, said, lifting his bonnet: "Weel, Majesty, the Hielanders put on their backs what the English folk put in their ballies." Jumping and foot-racing concluded the sports, the last race being over a long course and through the waters of the Dee, which caused much amusement and excitement.

Returning to the hotel I heard that there was to be a dinner, at which a large number of the Highlanders were expected to attend, and meeting Mr. Foggo, who inquired if I was going away, I said, "No, I intend to dine with the men," believing that it was a public dinner; to which he replied, "I am afraid you will find it rather a rough entertainment; but you will be thoroughly welcome." I found, therefore, that I was a self-invited guest, and had no cause to regret that I had obtained the privilege of attending the dinner and joining in the festivities as well as enjoying the good fare provided by Colonel Farquharson, and witnessing the novel and pleasing entertainment to which I had so unceremoniously invited myself. The dinner being concluded, Mr. Foggo, in brief but well-chosen words, gave first, the health of Her Majesty the Queen, which was responded to with all due enthusiasm, then followed the toast of the Earl of Fife, which was most cordially received, and many and hearty were the cheers that followed the short but cordial expressions of Mr. Foggo when proposing health and long life to the noble earl. But it was not until the toast of the evening was announced—the health of the Laird of Invercauld—that one realised the heartiness of Colonel

Farquharson's men, who received the toast with acclamation, shouting loudly, "with Highland honours." Thereupon every man jumped on his seat, placing one foot on the table; the glasses jingling and trembling, whilst the rafters rung with the lusty cheers, repeated again and again in the heartiest manner, speaking volumes for the popularity of their Highland chieftain. After heartily thanking Mr. Foggo for his kindness and attention I took leave of the festive party, and bent my steps homewards. By this time the moon had risen high, and

> Spreading herbs and flowerets bright
> Glistened in the dew of night.

The scenery was grand in the extreme seen by moonlight as we journeyed slowly over the mountainous pass, and the clock had chimed the hour of twelve long ere we reached the Manse. Quickly I sought my couch, tired with the pleasure and excited with the brilliancy of the gathering I had witnessed, and was soon far away in the land of dreams, answering a fancied inquiry as to what brought me, a stranger, to Braemar in the words of Fitzjames when confronting that stern and valiant chieftain, Rhoderick Dhu:

> Yet why a second venture try,
> A warrior thou, and ask me why?
> Moves our free course by such fixed cause
> As gives the poor mechanic laws!
> Enough, I sought to drive away
> The lazy hours of peaceful day,
> Slight cause will thence suffice to guide
> A knight's free footsteps far and wide ;
> A falcon flown, a greyhound strayed,
> The merry glance of mountain maid,
> Or if a path be dangerous known,
> The danger's self is ure alone.

CHAPTER VIII.

DEER-STALKING.

THERE is not a more exciting amusement than that of deer-stalking when followed in orthodox style. Then the sportsman must disregard toil and trouble, must possess skill and patience, be able to endure a vast amount of fatigue, and, lastly, he must be endowed with strong nerve, if he desire to bring down a big stag after a long and exciting stalk. A far different thing is a deer-drive: then, planted in a favourable position, the shooter—I cannot call him sportsman—may kill these noble animals without toil or trouble, skill or fatigue. This would to me be but a sorry representation of sport, and bears no comparison with the delight of trudging over the wild moorland, over the rugged hills, along the course of the brawling burn, in the endeavour to get within gunshot of the wary and crafty red-deer.

In order to show what value attaches to this description of sport, it is only necessary to point to the high prices which are paid for the so-called deer-forests. For instance, in Inverness-shire the large sum of 4960*l*. is paid for the privilege of enjoying the season's sport; whilst others are rented at various prices, 1760*l.*, 1500*l.*, and 1000*l.* being readily obtained by those entrusted with the management of Highland estates.

In Argyleshire a well-known forest is rented for the large sum of 4000*l.*; whilst 1840*l.*, 1000*l.*, and 800*l.* are amounts freely paid—I may say eagerly paid—for the opportunity of indulging in this fascinating amusement.

It is evident from the foregoing facts that deer-stalking is highly appreciated, and that it is beyond doubt a sport fit for kings, always provided that those seeking to try their hand at shooting the red-deer on their native hills and wild unfrequented haunts are endowed with the necessary qualifications for such an arduous pursuit, including an amount of patient perseverance under many difficulties and disappointments, a total disregard of the state of the elements, and beyond all a straight eye and a steady hand, without the possession of which no one must expect ever to rank high as a deer-stalker.

Amusing stories are told of persons who, after toiling for hours after a big stag, and at last getting within gunshot, have lost their nerve so utterly as to be unable to take aim until the object of their pursuit is careering far away, out of reach of the sportsman's bullet.

If a deer-forest is rented, the greatest care must be taken at the commencement of the season, lest by failing to study the wind or by careless shooting the deer are driven off the ground on to the neighbouring grouse-moor, the tenant of which will be on the look-out, and thus have a chance of shooting a stag or two.

In an early season the stags will be in full condition from the 20th August until the 10th September.

A sharp look-out has to be kept, in order to prevent the shepherds from adjoining sheep-walks disturbing the deer by running out their sheep, and frightening the herd with their dogs, who, being thus startled, will often clear right away from their pasture-ground, and seek some more remote spot where they can feed unmolested.

In winter these animals are seldom, if ever, fed, and in hard seasons die by scores. Being forced by hunger to come down to the low ground in search of food, they find their way to the sheep-troughs, and are pelted with stones by the shepherds and driven away, often to fall into the hands of poachers, who will shoot them even when out of condition, for the sake of their heads and horns. It would seem to be a very false economy on the part of owners of deer-forests not to make proper provision during the time when the snow covers the ground for many weeks together. The great secret of success in the working of a deer-forest is having a thoroughly good stalker who knows the favourite haunts of the deer, the state of the ground, and the condition of the locality—one whose practised eye can discern by examination of the slots of the animals the age, sex, and size of the deer which are upon the ground. In most cases there is not a tree or even a bush in the so-called deer-forests, which are created by withdrawing the sheep which have been fed on the land, and taking care that no one disturbs "the sanctuary" which is reserved for the pasturage of the red-deer. Good sport is often obtained on grouse-moors which adjoin deer-forests, as the deer frequently, when feeding up-wind, pass over the boundary, and are eagerly sought by the sportsman, who, tired of bringing down grouse, puts down his gun, and, rifle in hand, stalks the welcome visitor, and after some hours of hard labour, by dint of creeping on hands and knees over the rugged ground, stealing along the burns and round the mountainsides, finds himself within one hundred and fifty yards of a noble stag, and brings him down if he is fortunate, or, after all the toil and trouble, sees him career away, his bullet having missed its mark, causing much sorrow and vexation of spirit in the breast of the greatly disappointed sportsman.

An incident which occurred to a friend of mine will show the difficulties and uncertainties that beset the deer-stalker. After a long stalk over a most difficult country, my friend—who, by-the-way, is a marvellously good shot—succeeded in getting within easy distance of a fine stag. Taking steady aim, he fired at the deer, and to his delight saw him bound in the air, and then roll over and over down the mountainside to the level ground at the foot. Hastening in the company of the keeper to secure his prey, great was his dismay when he saw the stag rise from the ground and gallop away at full speed! It was supposed that, startled by the shot, the bullet perhaps just grazing him, he lost his balance, and thus toppled over from the height, the wonder being that he was not killed by the fall.

CHAPTER IX.

SALMON-FISHING.

ABERDEENSHIRE, Perthshire, and Inverness-shire are three of the best counties for the enjoyment of the entrancing sport of salmon-fishing. The Cluny river, which rises on the Cairnwall hill, wanders through a lovely country, eventually falling into the Dee at Braemar. The travellers journeying from the Spital of Glen Shee to Braemar will observe some beautiful pools, where, in the months of August and the early part of September, capital sport is obtained. A portion of this river—the Dee—belongs to Colonel Farquharson, of Invercauld, and visitors can obtain permission to fish certain parts of its waters, which are not very strictly preserved, by applying to the proprietor of the Invercauld Arms at Braemar. The upper reaches can only be fished by special permission. The Dee, which has its source amidst the summits of the Cairngorm Mountains, after winding through wild scenery of the grandest and most lovely description, finally falls into the German Ocean at Aberdeen.

The Dee is celebrated for its fine salmon-fishing, and the fish, though not running large, are yet exceedingly lively, showing excellent sport, requiring considerable skill on the part of the fisherman in order to land them safely out of the many rocky pools in which in due season they literally abound.

A portion of the Upper Dee is rented by Mr. Macnab, of the Fife Arms, Braemar, who has the exclusive right of fishing over seven miles of this beautiful river. Visitors residing at the Fife Arms are allowed to fish free of charge, and the right may be obtained by others on payment by the rod or month, according to arrangement.

At the time of writing this (May 1st) I hear of some wonderful sport on the Dee, two friends of Colonel Farquharson having recently landed no less than fourteen good salmon in one day.

The Don is also another river in Aberdeenshire that affords good sport, some very large salmon being taken at times. An amusing account was given me by Mr. Walker, Lord Petre's steward at Thorndon Park, himself a Scotchman, who, when a boy of ten years of age, saw a gentleman land a very heavy salmon from the Don. Looking admiringly at this monster of the deep, the gentleman said: "Would you like to take that fish home to your mother?" "Oh yes, sir," he promptly replied; and, catching hold of the salmon, he clasped it tight in his arms, and bent his steps homewards. After going a few yards, the salmon suddenly made such a vigorous movement that the boy fell head over heels, dropping the fish. Again and again he tried to carry off his prize, but each time was overthrown, and, after his third essay, he started off midst the laughter of those assembled, leaving the much-coveted fish on the ground.

The Beauly is the most noted river in Inverness-shire; it is a grand salmon-river, and is strictly preserved, though fishing is permitted in a limited part to those staying at the Beauly Hotel. Large rentals are obtained for the fishings on the noted rivers in Scotland, which are difficult to obtain, being always in great demand, salmon and trout fishing in the Highlands being sports which offer great attractions to a vast number of the disciples of Isaac Walton.

CHAPTER X.

HINTS ANENT HIRING MOORS.

No true sportsman can be considered to have thoroughly fulfilled his mission until he has enjoyed a season's grouse-shooting on the moors and climbed the mountains steep in order to bring down the ptarmigan on the Highlands of Scotland.

Partridge and pheasant shooting are certainly most enjoyable diversions, but they want the wild scenery, the large tracts of moorland, the difficult walking over the heather-clad hills, to make them rank with such sport as shooting grouse and ptarmigan, and, more than this, the bracing air which enables the sportsman to accomplish an immense amount of work over a difficult country without fatigue; a fact which was clearly established in my case when shooting over Rhidorach, the property of Colonel Farquharson of Invercauld, during last season. When I accepted the invitation I had little idea of the work I should be called upon to perform. Never having visited the Highlands of Scotland before, I was ignorant of the fact that the "shooting" over which I was to perform was to a great extent upon the Grampian Hills, my first view of which, when my attention was directed to the height to be attained before commencing work, was, to say the least, disheartening. "That's where we are to commence to-morrow," said my host, pointing to a spot some seven or eight hundred feet above the level of the winding road that leads from the Spital of Glen Shee to Braemar, running through the lovely valley of Glen Beg. I said but little, but thought the more, feeling convinced in my own mind that if I ever reached that height, it was as much as I should be able to accomplish; and as for walking over such a wild, mountainous, and rough country in pursuit of game, the idea seemed ridiculous, considering that I was not in training for walking, and was handicapped with the penalty of some sixty-five years. I felt that the attempt would end in a miserable failure. However, I determined to die game, and show that I was not a dunghill-bred one, and with this resolve I started on my first day's grouse-shooting. Before commencing the steep climb, however, I had to go down a declivity and cross a somewhat wide, swift-flowing burn. This was not an easy task, but I accomplished it, not, however, without some trouble, and then I began to ascend the hillside. By the time I had reached the height of five hundred feet I was breathless—dead beat, in fact—and sat down on a big boulder-stone, and thought what a fool I was to have imagined for a moment that I could walk over such ground. The Cairnwall, a mountain over 3500 feet in height, was pointed out to me as being the home of the ptarmigan, and I was told that part of the first day's beat was the side of this Grampian Hill, the summit of which I felt morally certain would never be reached by me, and that if the ptarmigan were only to be found at such high altitudes, I should never see those beautiful birds, however I might get on with the grouse on the lower level.

Aroused by the repeated calls of my companion, a man in the prime of life, his age being forty and his build herculean, who made light of the work—which, by-the-way, he was accustomed to—I held my tongue and toiled after him until, as I ascended higher and higher, I found, to my astonishment, that the feeling of fatigue was passing away, that I had gained my second wind, and was able to walk the remainder of the day without fatigue. It is evident that there must be something marvellous in the properties of the Highland atmosphere to allow of a person of my age walking day after day over moor and mountain for ten or eleven hours. Such, however, was the case; and I climbed Cairnwall, Glas Muol (or Miele), Ben Gouliping, Cairn Yourn, and most of the other mountains which travellers from Blairgowrie to Braemar see as they journey from the Spital of Glen Shee down Glen Beg to the watering-place at which the coaches stop, known as the Queen's Well, near the Devil's Elbow, a point which no one will be likely to forget who has ever travelled that way, for certain it is that a more ugly turn cannot be imagined than that which the coaches have to be tooled round. Here I can give the sportsman a hint, should he never have walked over the Grampian Hills before, which may be useful and conduce greatly to his comfort in walking: it is to take special care to provide himself with several pairs of boots, not too thick or heavy, well studded with nails, and fitting truly, and to wear them into shape before he commences work. Heavy, clumsy, clodhopper's boots are a mistake, and only tire the wearer, and are apt to chafe the feet where there is a wrinkle; whereas light boots of pliable leather will be far more comfortable, and can be rendered thoroughly waterproof if well dressed with dubbin.

Of course the intending sportsman will peruse the pages of "The Sportsman's Guide," in which he will find a long list of moors, deer-forests, and salmon-fishings which are to let; particulars being published by Mr. J. Watson Lyall, of 15, Pall Mall, of properties, the rentals ranging from 5*l.* to 4000*l.*, and even more. However, with foresight and judgment in the selection of a moor, a fair amount of sport may be obtained at a cost of 400*l.* or 500*l.* per annum; but prior to concluding a bargain for this description of property, the tenant proposing to rent a moor should walk over the ground and make inquiries as to the head of game, and who last shot over it. If the occupier was a sportsman he will probably find that a fair stock of breeding birds has been left; if a pot-hunter has rented it, doubtless he will find few but old birds remaining, as your pot-hunter goes in for numbers, and slaughters every bird, big or little, old or young, that comes in his way; and it is only the wary old cocks and antiquated hens that escape his murderous gun.

Having secured his shooting, the next consideration must be his dogs. My experience tells me that black-and-tan Gordon setters are the best sort of dogs for Highland work, being hardy and able to stand the severe climate, and capable of doing any reasonable amount of work. Having judiciously selected his moor, and provided a good team of dogs, he may, especially if he has the good fortune to fall in with a clever and willing keeper, look forward hopefully for a good season's sport when the glorious 12th of August arrives.

One further hint I will venture to give: that is, to use the Schultze gunpowder in preference to the ordinary black powder. The combustion is quicker and more complete; consequently there is far less smoke. Sometimes the sight of the bird is obscured when firing the second barrel on a dull heavy day, the smoke of the black powder hanging about and hindering the shooter from taking ready aim.

With regard to the selection of guns, the number of different sorts being legion, Purdey of course ranks amongst the highest and best of the many makers, and from his stock the sportsman can obtain whatever style he thinks will suit him best without fear of disappointment. My attention was recently drawn to an article in *Land and Water* (April 22nd) on an improvement in what is called by Messrs. Silver the "automatic" safety bolt as applied to a hammerless gun, and upon examination subsequently of the gun I came to the conclusion that it fulfilled all the conditions pointed out by the writer in that paper. A large selection of guns of every sort can be seen also at E. M. Reilly & Co.'s establishment in Oxford Street, and the intending purchaser will be difficult to please if he cannot suit himself at one or other of these noted makers.

CHAPTER XI.

AN IMPERIAL HUNTRESS.

I.

A KEEN air was blowing, and a heavy mist veiled the landscape, as I drove rapidly along on Saturday, on my way to the meeting of Sir Watkin Wynn's celebrated pack of hounds, which was fixed for Macefan, the residence of the Hon. Edward Kenyon, five miles from Whitchurch, in the county of Shropshire. The hour named was half-past ten; and it was evident that the desire to see the Empress of Austria in the field was uppermost in the mind of the dwellers in this part of Salop. Horses and carriages were at fabulous prices, every available vehicle and every possible horse being requisitioned for this important occasion. Commenting rather strongly on prices for vehicular conveyance, I was met with the old familiar rejoinder that it was not so much the paucity of horses as the rarity of the presence of an empress in this somewhat primitive part of the world that sent up prices to so high a point. Trotting smartly along, we passed many well-mounted men, some in scarlet with green collars, the uniform of the hunt; several ladies, who looked as if they were well accustomed to face a big fence or the occasional tall banks, and old hawthorn hedges, which are the characteristics of this country. Arriving at Macefan, I found Charles Payne, who has hunted Sir Watkin Wynn's hounds for the last fifteen or sixteen years, with nineteen and a half couples of useful hounds, which showed evident signs of hard work, being rather fine drawn, though looking fit to go the pace, as I found they could do. Awaiting the arrival of the pack, we paraded in front of the house, out of the way of the immense crowd that had assembled in an adjoining field, through which it was arranged that the imperial huntress should pass, so that the many who had travelled from far and near might look upon the royal visitor. Sir Watkin Wynn's hounds hunt the extensive district around Wrexham, Ellesmere, Whitchurch, and Oswestry four days a week, and are kennelled at Wynnstay, near Ruabon, in Denbighshire, and have a world-wide reputation as one of the crack packs of the country. Sixty couples of hounds are maintained, in order to show sport to the inhabitants of this district. The whips, J. Blower and W. Pinder, were well mounted, and looked neat and efficient workmen. Close to time the Empress, attended by several of her suite, drove up, and, having alighted, entered the house. The clever-looking bay thoroughbred horse which had been selected to carry her majesty was quickly brought up to the door, and, after a short delay, this ardent votaress of the chase proceeded to mount her steed, whilst her grooms were instructed by her to alter the saddle to suit her requirements. In immediate attendance were Sir Watkin Wynn and Captain Middleton, who pilots her majesty on such occasions; nor could any better man be found, being a first-rate performer across country. From her graceful seat, and the way in which she handled her reins, it was evident at a glance that the Empress is an accomplished horsewoman. The nag selected as her first mount appeared at first sight to be rather slight, but as the Empress is a light weight, riding only about nine stone, there was no doubt that the thoroughbred could carry her in proper form. The dark-blue habit, having a trimming of fur round the collar, was perfection, fitting her elegant figure with the utmost precision, not a crease nor a wrinkle being observable, and cut to the precise length that a well-made habit should be. Then Captain Middleton leads the way, and the Empress, followed closely by Sir Watkin Wynn, entered the paddock, looking at the hounds and addressing the huntsmen in gracious and pleasant style. Prior to the hounds being thrown into cover there was time to observe the large number of persons assembled, riders and lookers-on, among whom I noticed Lord Combermere and Lady Paget, Lord and Lady Rocksavage, the Hon. Edward Kenyon of Macefan, Mr. Hayward Lonsdale, Major Bulkeley, Captain Beatty, Captain Cote, Mr. Poole of Marbury, Mr. Oliver Ormerod, Mr. Cross of Wirswall, Mr. and Mrs. Briggs, Mrs. Godsell and Miss Thompson, Mr. Hill (well known with the North Shropshire hounds), Mr. Reginald H. Corbet (Master of the South Cheshire hounds), Captain Baldwin, Mr. Parker, Messrs. Harrison, etc. — Churton Vernon, Mr. Richard Cox, of Malpas, Master Black, and a host of others hailing from far distances. Then the hounds were trotted off to a cover close at hand, which, it was said, was sure to hold a fox. Payne promptly throws them into the gorse, and "Halloo! halloo! yo have at him!" such

are the sounds that we hear. While the hounds are
busy in their endeavour to find a fox, the Empress
rides quietly to the coverside, and an opportunity is
afforded to everyone of seeing and admiring this
distinguished huntress. In a very few minutes the
welcome cry of "Tally ho! tally ho! Gone away,
gone away!" is heard, and there is a rush of horsemen,
all endeavouring to get a good start. Piloted by
Captain Middleton, the Empress gets through the
crowd, and goes away at a rattling pace, taking the
fences in right good form. The bay is excited, and
starts at a tremendous pace, seeming as if he would
get the better of his rider, but the Empress is equal
to the occasion. Pulling him together, and turning
him round, and being thus cleverly steadied, he goes
in proper form during the remainder of the run. The
fox goes in the direction of Carton, and then makes
for the Bickerton Hills; afterwards doubling back, he
returns to the cover at Macefan, but is not allowed to
remain there long, and breaks cover again this time
across the vale, where the ground is deep and holding,
making for the Wyches, and thence in the direction
of Malpas, when the hounds were lifted to a "Halloo!"
at the fox having been viewed crossing the Whitchurch Road. I was able to take a note of the field,
a very small portion of those who started being with
Payne when he made a cast, and got again on the line
of the fox, who led them a merry and somewhat circuitous dance of fully two hours over a stiff line of
country—a run, however, that was nevertheless entirely
satisfactory, and thoroughly enjoyed by the royal visitor.
Of the Empress's skill as a horsewoman there can be
no difference of opinion, and of her love of fox-hunting

there is still less doubt, as shown by her energetic mode of proceeding, having hunted three days in succession, after a long and tedious journey. By constant exercise and, I am told, by a regular course of gymnastics, a state of health is maintained which enables her to ride long distances, and to enjoy without fatigue her favourite sport. Those who witnessed the management of her horse on this occasion could not doubt her nerve, and those who followed her over this difficult country could not fail to admire her skill and judgment in riding to hounds. I have seen many ladies who ride boldly and gracefully to hounds—notably Lady Grey de Wilton and Mrs. Sloane Stanley, whose performances across the broad pastures of Leicestershire are well known to all frequenters of Melton; but it is no flattery to say that for elegance of style, undaunted courage, beautiful seat, and light hands, the Empress of Austria is not to be excelled by any one of our boldest and hardest riding horsewomen.

Combermere Abbey is situated within four miles of Whitchurch, and great is the satisfaction of the tradesmen of this quiet town at the fact of the Empress having selected their locality for enjoyment of hunting, instead of again visiting Ireland, as originally intended. It was not clever on the part of the inhabitants of that country to have driven away so distinguished a visitor. The large expenditure of her establishment would, I should have thought, been valuable, but as the fashion of "Boycotting" those who rode the hounds in certain counties was adopted, it became necessary to change the venue, and hence the selection of this part of Shropshire, where opportunities offer of riding with five different packs of high-class hounds, over a good though stiff country, where foxes abound and good sport is generally shown. The number of hunters for her majesty's own use that have been brought over is ten, thirty-five are provided for the suite and servants, and some ten or twelve carriage-horses, whilst the total number of the suite and servants, I am told, is no less than eighty. Little doubt that, from the tradesmen's point of view, such an invasion is looked upon with complaisance. Should there be no fixture to-morrow, I hope to have a look at Combermere Abbey, which, I am told, is well worth seeing, being situate in a beautiful country, and well placed for hunting, as hounds can always be reached within reasonable distances.

On Tuesday the hounds will meet within a short distance of the Abbey, when I hope to have another opportunity of seeing the imperial huntress go across country. It is expected that a great number will attend the meet on that day. The term for which the occupation of the mansion has been arranged is six weeks, at the expiration of which time the hunting season will be drawing to a close. The cold winds, productive of many pecks of dust, which are stated to be worth a king's ransom, are, nevertheless, great drawbacks to sport, since when the wind is in the east it is neither good for man nor fox-hunting. As regards the market-town of Whitchurch, which is distant from London some one hundred and eighty-three miles, it may be truly said that it is a quiet—nay, even rather a sleepy—locality in which to pass a lifetime; eminently businesslike and respectable, though a trifle dull; old-fashioned as to its streets and buildings, but boasting a fine old church. It also boasts a remarkable monument to John Talbot, first Earl of Shrewsbury, surnamed the English Achilles, who was killed at the battle of Bordeaux. His bones were transferred from France and interred at Whitchurch. The police arrangements of the district are under the direction of the chief constable, Captain Harrison, and Superintendent Plant, as well as the chief superintendent of the Shropshire constabulary, Mr. Haines, who unostentatiously perform their duties, whilst showing themselves courteous to all comers who require information.

II.

CHILL blew the wind, with a bitter accompaniment of sleet, as I galloped along *en route* for Combermere Abbey on Monday morning. A gray mist partially veiled the country, causing the venerable oaks and ancient hawthorns to stand prominently in the gloom. There was no fixture within a moderate distance of Whitchurch, and therefore, not having the opportunity of riding to hounds, I determined to visit the Abbey, in order to see the residence selected for the Empress of Austria during her temporary sojourn in this country for the purpose of enjoying the pleasures of the chase. Gradually the mist cleared away, and I was able to form an opinion of the nature of the locality. I saw a wide expanse of undulating land, principally grass, over which the going was delightful. To ride across this country at the tail of a pack of fleet hounds requires a clever, bold, and resolute horse, if the rider wishes to go the pace and take a place in the first flight. Inquiring my way, I was directed to a lodge of which no other portion was visible save the door and window, the remainder being covered with a dense mass of tangled ivy. I trotted along through an extensive plantation, where weird and knotted oaks and moss-covered hawthorns were the principal features. Emerging from this woodland, I soon came in sight of the Abbey, a pile of ancient buildings having no architectural pretensions, placed in a sheltered hollow on the bank of a large lake or mere, of some hundred and fifty acres in extent. It did not appear a very inviting place for a winter residence, but being in the centre of an excellent hunting country, the object the Empress had in view is sufficiently attained. Referring to Camden, I find that "Cumbremere Abbey was founded and endowed in 1133 by Hugh Malbanc, Lord of Namptwich, for Cistercians." In Camden's time it belonged to "Sir Robert Salusbury Cotton, Bart." Further, I read that "A mile from Cumbermere Abbay in time of mind sunk a piece of hill having trees on hit, and after in that part sprang salt water, and the Abbat there began to make salt, but the men of the Wyches componed with the Abbay that there should be no salt made." Many additions and alterations have been made in the Abbey to render it suitable for its distinguished tenant; one room has been specially set aside as a gymnasium, where the necessary apparatus has been erected, and it is here that her majesty takes daily exercise for an hour. An extensive range of stabling, placed at some distance from the mansion, affords accommodation for the large stud which has been brought over from Austria. On arriving at the house I found that, as there was no meet within easy distance, her majesty was employing her time in taking horse exercise, galloping across the park, and visiting the training-ground that has been laid out for the exercise of the stud. Hurdles have been set up, and banks and fences made, over which the Empress rides in order to keep herself in good practice. After galloping round the park, I crossed over the bridge that spans a narrow part of the mere, pulling up to observe the many coots and divers that were disporting themselves on the bosom of the lake.

On Tuesday the meet of the South Cheshire Foxhounds was arranged for Goldbourne's Farm, Wilkesley, one of their best fixtures. When I looked out at daybreak I found a heavy fall of snow had covered the roofs of the houses. As the morning advanced the snow-fall increased, until it was evident that there could be but little sport, even if the hounds should put in an appearance; and as there was a distance of nearly seven miles to be traversed ere Wilkesley was reached, I decided that it would be a waste of time and energy to attempt gaining the trysting-place; an opinion which was shared by several sportsmen who had travelled a considerable distance by train to join in the chase. A message had been despatched to Mr. Corbet, conveying the intelligence that the Empress would not attend the meet in consequence of the severity of the weather, which rendered riding to hounds both difficult and dangerous.

After drawing for some time a fox was eventually found in Wilkesley Cover, which went away in the direction of Audlem; giving those who were hardy enough to ride on such a dismal day, and over ground

AN IMPERIAL HUNTRESS.

in such a heavy state, a tolerably satisfactory gallop, amongst whom Lord Rocksavage, Lord Combermere, Major Buckley, Mr. Tollemache, and some other *habitués* of the hunt were found enjoying their favourite pastime in spite of the foul weather.

The snow having ceased for awhile, the Empress sallied forth to Wilkesley cover, but the hounds had found and gone away at a rattling pace, and as the snow once more descended thickly, her majesty bent her steps homewards. This day (Thursday) the Empress is expected to be present at the Hunters' Steeplechases, at Ash, near Whitchurch, having subscribed the liberal sum of 200*l*. towards the stakes. Should the weather be fair, a very large concourse of spectators is expected on the course.

It is believed that Her Imperial Majesty will honour Mr. and Miss Tollemache with a visit for a few days at Dorfold Hall, in North Cheshire, where an opportunity will be afforded of riding with the Cheshire Hounds, of which Captain Park Yates is the well-known master. This noted pack hunts the district around Northwich, Chester, and Tarporley four days a week, no less than fifty couples of high-class hounds being required to enable Captain Yates to satisfy the requirements of this extensive district.

Afterwards her majesty, it is stated, will pay a brief visit to Baron Schröder, at The Rookery, near Nantwich. The Empress will also take an opportunity of riding with the North Staffordshire Foxhounds, of which the Marquis of Stafford is master, hunting the district around Stafford, Stoke-upon-Trent, and Crewe. This pack consists of sixty couples of grand hounds and the district over which they hunt is very wide, the kennels being at Trentham, the pack hunting four days a week. It will be seen, therefore, that abundant opportunity offers for our illustrious visitor to enjoy her favourite pastime nearly every day in the week during her stay in this country.

CHAPTER XII.

A ROYAL STAG-HUNT.

> To brightest beams distracted clouds give way,
> So stand thou forth—the time is fair again,

Were the words I addressed to one of my sporting companions on the morn of the day which had been fixed for the visit of His Royal Highness the Prince of Wales to the lovely counties of Devon and Somerset, for the purpose of witnessing, for the first time, the exciting sport of chasing the wild red-deer over the heather-clad hills, through the emerald glades, the densely-shaded coombes, the wild and romantic spots which are to be found in and about Exmoor. All that was needed to make the visit enjoyable to the Prince was fair weather; but so wild and wet had been the spring, summer, and autumn, as far as we had entered upon it, that scarcely anyone ventured to predict a fine day. A friend of mine, whose temper has been sorely tried, and whose ideas have been sadly muddled by the novel system of weather forecasts, inquiring of me how I accounted for these wonderful climatic disturbances, I replied that it had been well known for a long period that the sun had been under a cloud, and

the elements having assembled, it was resolved that
"Sol" should go into liquidation; hence these tears,
or, more properly speaking, tempestuous times. Better
fortune, however, was in store for us, and

> Soon as the morning trembles in the sky,
> And unperceived unfolds the spreading day,

I am up, anxiously watching for the coming dawn, and
I see

> The quenchless stars, so eloquently bright;
> Untroubled sentries of the shadowy night,

pale away, and retire before the jocund morn. For
once in a way we were to have bright sunshine, calm-
breathing breezes, and pleasant weather throughout
an entire day. The Prince of Wales had travelled
on Thursday last from Devonport to the Dunster
Station, by rail, arriving at that singularly quaint old
town at 5.25 P.M. An immense concourse of spectators,
hailing from all parts of Devon and Somerset, were
eagerly awaiting a sight of the Heir Apparent, who
had never previously visited this, the fairest portion of
his dominions. Upwards of a hundred tenants of the
Dunster Castle estate, on horseback, were in waiting
to escort the Prince through the town, which was
gaily decked with flags, evergreens, and flowers;
whilst the assembled multitude cheered the royal
visitor to the very echo. With little loss of time the
cavalcade reached the Castle, a venerable pile of
buildings, erected on a tor, from which there are very
extensive views of the adjacent lovely country, with
the noble range of the Quantock Hills, which trend
down to the Bristol Channel, as a background. The

Castle was erected by Sir William de Mohun, one of
the noblest of the host who accompanied William the
Conqueror to England. The Luttrells of Dunster
Castle, his descendants, are now represented by Mr.
George Fownes Luttrell, a large landowner, a Master
of Foxhounds, and a thorough sportsman. A large
and select party of visitors were invited, including
Prince Louis of Battenberg, Viscount and Viscountess
Bridport, the Hon. Rosa Hood, Lord Ebrington, Rear-
Admiral Hood, C.B., Mr. and Mrs. Granville Somerset,
Colonel Kingscote, Sir Henry Keppel, Lord Charles
Beresford, Mr. Alexander Luttrell of the Rifle Brigade,
the Rev. John Russell, Mrs. Bosanquet, and Mr.
Knollys, etc. Twenty-seven guests in all sat down
to an elegant banquet in the truly baronial hall.

Knowing that there would be little chance of
obtaining accommodation at either Dunster, Porlock,
or Minehead, I journeyed to my favourite quarters,
the Lion Hotel, at Dulverton; and on my arrival there
I found every room engaged and every horse and
carriage bespoke. In fact, so great was the demand,
that, rather than be disappointed of the sight, one
gentleman amongst the many seeking in vain for the
means of reaching the meet on the following morning
at Hawkcombe Head, telegraphed to London for horses
to be sent down. Having taken the precaution of
ordering a horse some days previous, I found the
following morning, at the appointed hour of eight
o'clock, a sturdy cob brought round to the door, upon
which I mounted and trotted away smartly, having
eighteen miles to go to cover, travelling for some time
along the bank of the River Barle, which was brawling
loudly, as its sparkling waters hurried over the big

boulders on their way to join the Exe. Away up the steep hills, through the narrow lanes, stopping to pick a spray of the beautiful wild honeysuckle, which drooped gracefully from the tall hedgerow, admiring the innumerable beautiful ferns that deck the banks, and the beautiful foxgloves peeping out from amidst them. Then Winsford Hill is reached, from which there is a glorious view over the vast space of undulating ground, visible as far as Dartmoor.

At this season of the year the country usually presents a brilliant appearance, the lovely hues of the heather-bloom being the chief feature; this year of cheerless weather, however, has sadly changed the aspect of hills and dales, scarcely a handful of blossom being visible. Then as I cantered quickly along I overtook numbers of horsemen, and many in carriages, carts, and waggons, hastening to Hawkcombe: then Exford was reached, where I halted for five minutes. This place I found crowded, and I was prepared by the signs on the road to find that Devon and Somerset had come out literally in their thousands, clustering on every hillside along the route which the Prince was expected to traverse on his way to the fixture. The pack, consisting of fifteen couples of fine hounds, was on the hillside surrounded by a group of well-known sportsmen, amongst whom were Mr. S. H. Warren of Dulverton, the acting Master in the absence of Mr. Mordaunt Fenwick Bissett, whose absence was regretted greatly, more especially as it was caused by the very recent death of his father, Archdeacon Bissett; Mr. Froude Bellew, the Master of the well-known Dulverton Foxhounds, and Mrs. Bellew, one of the boldest and best riders it has ever been my good fortune to see; Dr. Collyns, accompanied by his nephew, who, following the footsteps of his uncle, will keep up the reputation of this sporting family, if I mistake not; Earl Fortescue; Sir Thomas Dyke Acland, a large landowner, and a staunch supporter of stag-hunting, who, though never joining in the sport himself, could not refrain on this occasion from making one of the number assembled to do honour to the Prince, doing everything in his power to ensure success, especially in case the stag should run in the direction of Cloutsham, and over Dunkery, the highest point on the coast of the Bristol Channel, upon which the warning beacon stands that guides the mariner up and down this dangerous passage; Mr. Nicholas Snow, the Master of the celebrated pack of foxhounds known as the "Stars of the West;" Mr. Chorley, the Master of the Dulverton Harriers; Mr. and Mrs. Connack Marshall; the Rev. John Jekyl and Miss Jekyl; and a host of well-known residents and riders of this part of the country, including Mrs. Collyns, Mrs. S. H. Warren, Mrs. Williams, and many others who, from want of space, I am unable to enumerate. In the midst of his pack, mounted on a clever-looking horse, was Arthur Heal, the well-known huntsman, successor to the renowned "Jack Babbage" who hunted the Devon and Somerset for many years, whose quiet demeanour and manner attracted the especial attention of His Royal Highness; with George Southwell, the cheery whip and hard rider over this extremely difficult country; and Miles the Harbourer in attendance, whose province is to track the stag, denoting his whereabouts—a most important person in the

proceedings, as he it is we depend upon to find us a
"runable" stag on this momentous occasion. Then,
whilst the large assemblage are picnicing and enjoying
themselves, a loud and protracted cheer announces
the arrival on the scene of the royal visitor, who,
in a carriage-and-four, passed at slow pace along the
line of spectators, who, waving hats and handkerchiefs,
welcomed their Prince with loud huzzas. Accompanying
His Royal Highness was Prince Louis of Battenberg,
Mr. Luttrell, the Rev. John Russell (the octogenarian
sportsman, so well known and deeply respected in
these parts), and Lord Charles Beresford. After
leisurely passing through the line of lookers-on and
halting frequently, enabling all present to see him
to advantage, the carriage moved on to the stables
of the hunt, where Mr. Prince, the stud-groom, was
in waiting with the Prince's two favourite hunters,
Cockney and Dashwood, who carried him safely over
flood and field during his visit to India. Then, His
Royal Highness having mounted, Arthur Head, with
three couple of tufters, proceeded to draw for a stag
in Lord Lovelace's beautiful covert, which runs down
in the direction of the seashore. The view from this
point was lovely in the extreme; across the Channel
was the Welsh coast, seemingly basking in the brilliant and welcome sunshine which favoured us this day;
before us was Bossington Point, a bluff, bold head-
land, overlooking Porlock Bay; to the right the grand
heather-clad hill of Dunkery; and on the hillsides,
and upon every "coign of vantage," a serried host of
spectators.

Ere long the horn of the huntsman is heard on the
hill; there is a quickened movement on the part of the

phalanx of horsemen assembled at the farther end of the wood; then the welcome cry of "Tally ho! tally ho!" is heard, as a fine stag is seen crossing the open space, going in the direction of Porlock; but, fearing to face the open, he returns to his favourite home amidst the leafy shades, turning out one of his younger companions from his lair, and quietly taking his place, as is the cunning custom of the wild red-deer when pursued by his foes, for we see a fresh and lighter stag moving in the woodland wild. Then again we hear loud and repeated cries of "Tally ho!" from the crowd, and gallop away in hot haste, making for Exmoor. Here we are doomed to disappointment, for it is a young stag, and Mr. Warren does not allow the hounds to be laid on the scent. Then we make our way down a tremendously steep hill, through a babbling stream, along a lovely valley, mounting another hill, and going in the direction of Deer Park—a portion of moorland in the vicinity of Oare Valley, especially reserved and carefully fenced in as a preserve for the red-deer by the owner, Mr. Snow, who is one of the greatest supporters of this unique and manly pastime. Very soft was this treacherous grass-grown part of the moor, soddened as it had been by the long and penetrating rains, and my sturdy brown cob was suddenly floundering up to his hocks in a boggy place, from which, however, he cleverly extricated himself without much difficulty.

"Keep moving, sir," said a well-mounted farmer; "this is a very soft spot, and it doesn't do to stand still." Frequently as I have gone across this country, I have never known it to ride so badly, and when crossing at full speed over that part in which deep trenches had been cut for the purpose of drainage, it was due to the cleverness of the animal I was mounted on that I was saved from coming to grief whilst crossing these grass-grown, rotten pitfalls. A short time had only elapsed when a stag went away, going in the direction of a grand line of country, and we tallied him in vain, for there were several stags and hinds on foot; but at last one broke away from the coombe, and went away at a rattling pace, and, the hounds being promptly laid on, we were soon urging on our steeds through the boggy ground, rising precipitous ascents or descending the almost perpendicular hillsides, crossing swiftly-flowing rivulets, stumbling over the big boulders, but still going on, on, in pursuit of our quarry. At one time I saw three men down at a grip, their horses sinking deep in the quagmire, one of the fallen losing a valuable gold watch in the mud. There goes the Prince, pounding along right well over hill and dale and moorland, making good way over the treacherous ground, when suddenly his horse sinks deep into the bog, and, floundering about for a moment, cleverly extricates himself, and is soon seen mounting one of the steep hills, bearing his rider safely to the summit, where the Prince halted for a moment to get a breather, whilst most of the riders had dismounted in order to ease their nags when climbing this steep acclivity. Then after crossing Doone Valley, and struggling across the forest, we cross the road and run in the direction of Lynton. Here the ground is firm and the going better. The field had by this time been greatly reduced by the pace and the difficult line which the stag had taken; then, after running within a short distance of Lynton, he doubles back and returns over the hills, making for Badgworthy Waters, where he is finally run into and killed. The Prince, who was well up at the finish, quickly dismounted and waded across the stream, and after witnessing the customary ceremonies attendant on the death of "the some time monarch of the glen," expressed himself greatly delighted with the run, which lasted for one hour and forty-five minutes. Only a select few were able to live close to the hounds throughout this capital chase. Conspicuous amongst them was Mr. Collyns on his clever little gray horse, one of the best and most earnest of the many good sportsmen who ride with the Devon and Somerset; Mr. Chorley, the well-known Master of the Harriers, which show such fine sport over the heather; and Mr. Pearse. The Prince, leaving his escort and dispensing with the guidance of his pilots, "ganged his ain gate" for awhile, mingling with the farmers, and delighting them with his affability and good-humour, chatting freely about the country and the noble sport he had witnessed.

"Ah Prince," said one, "you're no bad judge of a horse," when he told them that he had bought the nag he was riding out of a baker's cart in the Isle of Wight.

Mr. Collyns was then presented to his Royal Highness, for the purpose of offering for acceptance a copy of "Notes on the Chase of the Wild Red-deer in the Counties of Devon and Somerset," written by his father, the well-known sportsman of former days, Charles Palk Collyns, a rare work, which gives the author's experience, during forty-six years, of the mysteries of "harbouring, tufting, and slotting the red-deer," which the Prince graciously accepted.

Earl Fortescue, Mr. Nicholas Snow, the Rev. John Russell, and several others were, if not in the very first flight, there or thereabouts during this clinking and now historical run. Great credit is due to that most genial of sportsmen, Mr. S. H. Warren, for his admirable management, as also to Sir Thomas Dyke Acland, Mr. Snow, and in fact to all the landlords and tenant-farmers of the district over whose ground the Prince of Wales first gained his experience of hunting the wild red-deer.

On Saturday afternoon the Prince terminated his brief visit, returning by rail to Devonport. A rare day of sunshine in this gloomy time caused the thousands present to have a most enjoyable time; but the weather the following day returned to its evil courses—a soaking rain and heavy mist blurring the beautiful landscape. One consequence of this sunless season is the want of the customary bloom on the heather, which usually at this season is the glory of the country. Scarcely a handful is to be gathered where, in other seasons, I have ridden for miles knee-deep amidst its beautiful blossoms. Never in my experience have I seen the country in so deplorable a state; all along the route from London to Somersetshire the hay is to be seen rotting on the ground or floating on water; a vast proportion of the grass still remaining uncut. In the lowlands the floods are out, the rivers are lakes, and the usually placid streamlets are now brawling brooks; the wheat in many places is badly laid, scarcely showing a yellow tint; here and there a sickly-looking crop of oats has been cut, and the sheaves hang down their heads in a despondent fashion. There is scarcely any fruit—here and there a few pears, no apples, plenty of green leaves, but few flowers, and those wearing a washed-out appearance. A more melancholy prospect for farmers I have never known; it is too late for recovery; without sunshine neither wheat, barley, nor oats can have any quality, and what hay is gathered must necessarily be inferior. The earth is literally soddened, and it required some considerable nerve to gallop over the treacherous soil of Exmoor, where you may suddenly find your fleet career checked by an inglorious fall into one of the deep bogs, from which it is no easy matter to extricate yourself and horse.

CHAPTER XIII.

HOUNDS AND HORSES.

FROM all the great hunting centres the most satisfactory accounts are given of the sport enjoyed during this season, so far as it has gone. Scarcely a day has been lost up to the present time; the frosts that have been experienced, though severe whilst they lasted, have been of the briefest. Several weeks of dry, genial weather brought the ground into capital condition, the scent being greatly improved thereby; and all the crack packs in the kingdom have reason to boast of downright good sport and many clinking runs. Foxes, as a rule, are plentiful; the sport more popular, if possible, than ever, as proved by the large "fields" that attend the various meets of the three hundred and forty-two packs of hounds that hunt over the United Kingdom. "Men may come and men may go," but in my opinion hunting-men are as likely to "go on for ever" as any other class, the hereditary love of the chase being one of the most deeply-rooted feelings in the breast of a true Briton. It may be that the style of hunting the stag, the hind, the fox, and the hare is somewhat different from that of old times; but still the same inbred desire to indulge in the pleasures of the chase exists as strongly now in Englishmen of the present day as it did in those of the distant period alluded to.

At Melton there has been a considerable number of visitors. The Earl of Wilton has not visited Egerton Lodge as yet, being away on board his yacht, seeking in warmer climes to escape from the rigours of our variable climate. The numerous friends and admirers of this venerable sportsman will be glad to hear that he is in good health, and contemplates returning about the end of February or the beginning of March, when he will be found in the saddle once more. His fine stud is in rare form, and Martin, his lordship's stud-groom, may be depended upon to have them as "fit as fiddles" when his noble master once again joins in the sport which he has followed for so long a period. Looking back so far as 1837, I find in the "Quarterly Review," which contains a list of visitors then residing at Melton, the names of the Earl and Countess of Wilton as being residents. I believe that the period at which the Earl of Wilton first visited that fashionable locality dates considerably beyond half a century. With the exception of the well-known Mr. Little Gilmour, he alone, of all his contemporaries, is to be found enjoying his favourite sport with unabated ardour. Colonel Forester, who has had a few runs with hounds, going as boldly as ever, met with a slight accident the other day, and has left for Bretby Park for a week or two.

The best sport as yet has been shown by the Belvoir Hounds, which are hunted by Frank Gillard, one of the most persevering of huntsmen, who may always be depended upon to show sport if it is possible to do so. Those who wish to see a beautiful pack in superb condition and exhibiting the highest breeding, should not fail to have a look at the Duke of Rutland's hounds. Selecting the time when the fixture is at The Three Queens, anyone doing so will have a good opportunity of judging of their merits and riding across nice country, the going over which is easy, the fences always being practicable.

Tom Firr, the noted huntsman of the Quorn, had a bad fall, which has incapacitated him for awhile from carrying the horn. A somewhat similar mishap has befallen his first whip, who also is unable to be in his place, and the master, Mr. Coupland, has to hunt the hounds himself in the interim. Being a thorough sportsman as well as fine horseman, he will not fail to keep up the prestige of this famous pack. The Cottesmore, of which clipping pack Mr. Baird is the new master, have had some good runs, Neal doing his best on every occasion to kill his fox, and rarely failing to show good sport in that finest of all hunting countries.

In the Vale of Aylesbury Sir Nathaniel de Rothschild's staghounds have had some clipping runs; notably one a few days since, when the deer led them a merry dance over the big fields and tall fences of the Vale, being finally taken at a point seven miles beyond Buckingham, the hounds having to travel twenty-seven miles on their way home to the kennels at Ascott. Amongst those riding with this pack are the Hon. Robert Grimstone, the Earl and Countess of Clarendon, the Earl of Ilchester, the Hon. Rupert Carington, the Hon. K. P. Bouverie, Mr. John Foy, Messrs. Redfern, Gillat, Lucas, Chinnery, D'Avigdor, Marshall, and a host of hard-riding men. Mr. Leopold de Rothschild has entertained a succession of visitors, many of whom have joined in the sport. This fine pack of hounds will be found well worth a visit by anyone who wishes to see a brilliant lot of animals, to the perfection of which Fred Cox, who has hunted them for a quarter of a century, has devoted his time and attention. The success of his endeavours may be judged of by an inspection of the beautiful establishment at Ascott, near Leighton Buzzard. Capital stabling is to be had at the Hunt Hotel, close to the station, and every comfort will be found at that well-managed establishment. Those selecting this pleasant place for a residence will find no less than seven packs within easy reach, and may hunt, if they so desire, every day in the week. The Bicester foxhounds have had some clinking runs, and generally show grand sport when hunting in the Vale. The Whaddon Chase, of which Mr. W. Selby Lowndes is the master, also hunt in the vicinity of Leighton Buzzard, performing across the magnificent Vale of Aylesbury. Mr. Mordaunt Fenwick Bissett retires at the end of the season from the mastership of the Devon and Somersetshire Staghounds, having held that post for about twenty-five years, during which long period he has shown grand sport over those beautiful counties. Parliamentary duties necessitate his relinquishing the pleasures of the chase, and he will be succeeded by Viscount Ebrington, whose family have always been first and foremost in the support of the noble sport of hunting the wild red-deer, so popular throughout Devon and Somerset.

Those who have taken up their abode at Rugby have been favoured with capital sport with the Pytchley, the Atherstone, the North Warwickshire, and Sir Bache Cunard's hounds; notably the grand run from Braunston Gorse with the Pytchley, described by Goodall, who speaks with the experience of a lifetime devoted to the noble sport as being one of the very best that he can remember. This rattling run lasted over an hour, with only two slight checks, the hounds finally pulling down the stout old dog-fox that had shown them this fine day's sport. A very large "field" assembled on this occasion, but as the pace was very severe, the number living to hounds was soon reduced to reasonable limits. Mrs. Upperton and Mrs. Barton went extremely well; and Mr. Muntz—who, as usual, was in a good place—had the misfortune to kill his favourite chestnut-horse Hero, who fell at a double, breaking his back. Goodall, as usual, was in the right place throughout, and has the satisfaction of knowing that no hounds could have done their work better than the famous Pytchley pack. Sir Bache Cunard has had very good sport, and recently over the Billesdon Coplow country had a racing run that winnowed the "field" so thoroughly as to leave only seven or eight who were able to live with the hounds, consisting of the following well-known riders with this crack pack: Mr. Tailby, the late master; Mrs. Franklin, Sir B. Grant, Mr. Fernie, Mr. Logan, Mr. Allen, and Mr. Dunlop.

Travelling farther afield, an entirely different country is that hunted by the "Stars of the West," of which Mr. Nicholas Snow is the master, a thorough sportsman in every sense of the word, to whom the riders with the Devon and Somerset Staghounds are so largely indebted for the preservation of the wild red-deer in that portion of his estate dedicated specially to those noble animals. The country over which Mr. Snow hunts his hounds lies in the vicinity of Porlock, Lynton, Minehead, and Exmoor. There is nothing, in my opinion, more delightful than riding over this thoroughly wild tract of land, amidst some of the loveliest scenery that is to be found in England; listening to the music of the hounds as it is echoed and re-echoed from hill to hill; now galloping over the brown heather, climbing the steep ascents, fording the wide and swiftly-flowing streams.

The Dulverton Foxhounds, of which Mr. Froude Bellew is the well-known master, are kennelled at Rhyll, hunting the country around Dulverton, Winsford Hill, Tiverton, and South Molton. It is a thorough treat to ride with this fine sportsman, who has passed all his life amidst the beautiful scenery of North Devon, devoting much time to the pursuit of the stag and fox, and the bringing down of the many blackcocks that are seen winging their flight over his extensive tract of moorland. An opportunity was afforded, a few days since, of seeing how the Dulverton hounds do their work, when they found an exceedingly stout fox at Barkham Heath, on Lord Poltimore's North Molton estate, from whence they ran over the southwest part of Exmoor to Lanacre, then away to Hasgrove, over the Moorland of Winsford Hill to Hawkridge, killing their fox after a tremendous run extending over a distance of twenty miles.

The Surrey Staghounds have had capital sport. A recent run, said to be one of the best ever met with by those hunting with this clever lot of hounds, showed their power of endurance. The noted hind, Brown

Duchess, was uncarted a few days since at Norwood Hill, near Horley, and went away for twenty minutes, taking to the water, in which she remained for some time. The pace up to this point was terrific. Emerging from the waters of the brook in which she had refreshed herself, she went away at a racing pace, and was not captured until Daddles Hill, in Ashdown Forest, was reached, a distance of twenty-five miles from point to point. Out of a large "field" a few only were up at the finish, Hickman (the huntsman), Mr. John Percival, and Mr. Walter Norris being in time to secure Brown Duchess after this wonderful chase; Mr. W. Robinson (the late master), Mr. Wm. Morris, Mr. Geo. Morris, and Mr. W. H. Moore were the only other horsemen who lived throughout this remarkable run. The Surrey Staghounds are a very fine lot of animals, with great power and ability to stay, as this run proves; the deer are a fine lot, both stags and hinds being in first-rate condition, affording many clinkers over this varying country. That well-known sportsman, Mr. Richard Rawle, whose hounds hunt the country in the vicinity of Berkhampstead, has shown the followers of his clever pack of staghounds some very good runs; one, when a hind recently purchased from the herd which I saw taken a short time back in Thorndon Park, was uncarted, verifying a prediction I made, that it would take a good deal of time and all that noted sportsman's skill to capture her when turned out before his pack. The red-deer of the herd which Lord Petre has recently broken up are noted, Sir Nathaniel de Rothschild having several; and Boreham, who hunts Lord Carington's bloodhounds, tells me that he has had some of the same stock when Lord Wolverton hunted the Dorsetshire country. I am glad to be able to say that a considerable number of those captured in Thorndon Park are now in Weald Hall Park, where I saw them a few days since, quite at home in their new quarters. Masters of hounds should bear this in mind, as in time Mr. Christopher Tower will have to draft some of the extensive herd that he now possesses.

One of the consequences of the sad state of the "distressful country" has been an unworthy interference on the part of some of the Land Leaguers with the members of various hunts. Owing to the disturbances in the sister kingdom, the Empress of Austria has relinquished her intention of visiting Kilkenny, with the view of indulging in her favourite pastime. Sir Robert Harvey's brilliant pack of harriers has had some clinking good runs, one lasting considerably over an hour, the stout hare eventually being run into. Very fast are these well-bred hounds, and handsome as well, being derived from the pack of harriers belonging to Mr. Tom Mashiter, who sold them to his Royal Highness Prince Albert, at whose death they became the property of the Prince of Wales; and when his Royal Highness gave them up they were transferred to Sir Robert Harvey. When the fixture is in the vicinity of Harmondsworth, a rare day's sport may safely be depended on. Stout hares, open land, and easy fences are the characteristics of the neighbourhood; and many a clipping run have I enjoyed over that pleasant country in bygone days when Colonel, now Lord, Hood was the master.

So far the season has been an entire success. The heavy rains of the past few days will cause the land to ride very heavy, but with the coming of spring-time and open weather there will be found many noted packs which the ardent sportsman should not fail to visit. No man will have completed his education unless he has ridden to hounds in Yorkshire, and noted the workmanlike style in which the thing is done in that sporting county.

The Bedale, consisting of forty-eight couples of good hounds, hunt the country around Bedale, Thirsk, Ripon, and Northallerton; the master, Major F. H. Dent, carrying the horn. The Earl of Zetland's pack, consisting of fifty-five couples of stout, high-bred, handsome hounds, hunt the district around Croft, Tadcaster, Darlington, and Richmond regularly four days a week. The kennels are at Aske Hall, near Richmond, and the huntsman the well-known sportsman, T. Bridger Champion. The far-famed York and Ainsty makes up a quartet of first-rate packs, not to be surpassed by any in the kingdom.

Turning next to Lincolnshire, several crack packs will be found: first and foremost the Brockelsby, of which the Earl of Yarborough was the master. I speak in the past tense, having been told that he has retired; but, as rumour is not always strictly correct in its announcements, it is to be hoped that it has erred in this case. This noted pack hunts four days a week over the extensive district lying around Limber, Brigg, Caistor, Grimsby, and Market Rasen. The pack consists of fifty-three couples, and is hunted by Alfred Thatcher. The Burton Hunt, the headquarters of which are at Reepham, near Lincoln, can exhibit fifty-seven couples of noble hounds, hunting four days a week around Lincoln, Gainsborough, and Market

Rasen, showing first-rate sport. The dwellers in Lincolnshire, like those residing in Yorkshire, delight greatly in horses and hounds, producing some of the very best.

Drawing nearer to the metropolis, several good packs are to be found. The Oakley for one, hunting around Bedford, Sharnbrook, and Olney—a wide expanse of country—four days a week, having fifty-eight couples of excellent hounds to do the work. Easily reached from London, this old-established and first-rate pack should be seen. Many a fine day's sport have I witnessed with the Oakley in the days when Frank Beers hunted them. When the fixture is Shelton Gorse, let those who would like to see a downright good run try their luck there, and if, as usual, a stout old fox goes away, they will have no cause to regret the trouble of travelling so far. If space permitted, there are many other packs of hounds deserving notice, and it is clear to me that, notwithstanding the bad times, which have so largely affected the agricultural interest, neither the landlord nor tenant farmer has shown the least desire to interfere with the national sport of fox-hunting.

In respect to horses, it is evident that there is little decrease in the value of first-class animals, as proved in the recent sale, by Messrs. Tattersall, of Mr. Flower's fine stud, three out of the string realising the large sum of 1500 guineas, and the remainder highly satisfactory prices. Really good hunters, hacks, or harness-horses command as high prices as ever they did. Nevertheless, if you are prepared to open your purse-strings wide enough, and will visit Rugby, Acton, Green Street, Stamford Street, the Westminster Road, or other establishments of our well-known dealers, I will engage that you shall, with very little trouble, put together a string of first-class hunters that will carry you over any country in the United Kingdom. On former occasions I have spoken of the presence of ladies in the hunting-field; and gradually the attendance of the fair sex has increased until it has become an invariable rule that a number, many of whom ride thoroughly well to hounds, are found attending the fixtures of all the crack packs. Many of these votaries of Diana are well mounted, as they should be; but not unfrequently I observe ladies mounted upon brutes with heads like fiddle-cases, legs resembling those of a rocking-horse, and mouths as hard as a board of poor-law guardians. What a lady requires is a willing horse, with good temper, light mouth, courage if called upon to show it, and at the same time a perfect fencer, if she is to be carried well to hounds.

It will be seen by the foregoing particulars that hunting at any rate is not one of the pastimes of the country that is affected by the disturbed state of the political atmosphere, nor seriously influenced by the clouds now appearing in the horizon.

CHAPTER XIV.

SIR ROBERT HARVEY'S HARRIERS.

If your horse be well bred and in blooming condition,
   Up to the country and up to your weight,
Oh, then give the reins to your youthful ambition,
   Sit down in your saddle, and keep his head straight.

It was with a feeling of strong conviction that the above advice was thoroughly sound that I made up my mind to have a day with Sir Robert Harvey's Harriers, of which I have often heard very favourable reports, and with which, in bygone days, when they were the property of his Royal Highness Prince Albert, and were under the management of Colonel Hood, I have had many a rare good gallop in the neighbourhood of Windsor. Ascertaining that the fixture was at the village of Wraysbury, I requested Mr. Sherley, of Twickenham, to send on a favourite horse, which I have ridden on several occasions, and which I like better every time I get off him, and embarking on board a South-Western train, I journeyed to Staines, in order that I might go hunting the hare, as a pleasant pastime and agreeable occupation at this season of the year. Arriving at Staines, I promptly sought out the well-known establishment of Mr.

Stollery—the Railway Hotel—and confiding to the hostess of that well-managed hostelry that I needed refreshment before commencing the arduous duties of the day, and that I required merely the simplest fare—in fact, explaining that what little I took I liked to be of the best, I repaired to the stables to look after my steed. At that moment there appeared on the scene a pack of hounds, consisting of nine couples and a half of useful-looking animals, which upon inquiry, I found were the well-known lot of draghounds, now the property of Mr. Herbert Rymill, whose residence is in the vicinity of Staines, which Mr. Pitcher was taking out for a little exercise. These hounds, I am told, show rare sport to those who enjoy following a drag, every one being a foxhound, entered to this particular style of sport, and enabling those who ride to them to enjoy a right-down good gallop over a carefully-selected line of country. Intending on a future occasion to try my fortune with them, I retired to my hostelry and made a fierce onslaught on the roast-beef and other luxuries I found awaiting me, after which I mounted my steed, who was as fresh as paint and desirous of showing how thoroughly light-hearted he was, to which end he jumped about and disported himself so gaily that I thought it advisable to give him a breather across some of the meadows adjacent to the town. Having allowed him to play the wag for awhile, I trotted him away sharply until I reached Wraysbury Church, where I fell in with the hounds. Before, however, business commenced, Mr. Birch insisted that all the "field" should partake of his hospitality, and George Farr and his whip having retired with the pack to the stackyard, I had an opportunity, whilst the numerous guests of this hospitable sportsman were enjoying the good things placed before them, of looking over the eleven couples and a half of beautiful harriers forming the pack on this occasion. A remarkably even lot of well-bred animals are those of Sir Robert Harvey's, measuring eighteen inches only, but wonderfully fast, as subsequent proceedings showed, as well as steady and musical in their work. Time was afforded to observe those I knew amongst the visitors present—some seventy or more well-mounted men and five or six ladies, assembled to enjoy a day's hunting under the most favourable conditions; the day being perfectly lovely—bright, warm, with a westerly wind, bringing out the gnats, a strange change from the bitter cold of the few previous days. First to attract my notice was the master, Sir Robert Harvey, of Black Park, mounted on a good-looking chestnut, accompanied by his daughter, whose subsequent plucky performance I shall narrate in due course, riding a useful-looking bay. Then Mr. Scott, the active secretary, who has for many years used every exertion to obtain success and subscribers—for this is a subscription pack—which exertions, by-the-way, are fully appreciated and acknowledged by the many gentlemen who for years have belonged to the hunt; Mr. Peter Fowler, a staunch supporter, over whose land these hounds roam whenever they please, being always certain of sport whenever they visit the farm of this thorough sportsman, who is ever ready to give a hearty welcome to all-comers when the fixture is at his homestead; Mr. Harris, of Staines, on a sturdy bay cob; Mr. Mavor, riding a handsome chestnut, rising five years old, whose eager behaviour kept his rider well employed to control his anxiety to be first and foremost in the flight; Mr. Willet, jun., of Wyke, riding a remarkably clever cob, the property of Mr. Farnell Watson, who, many of those riding with his crack pack of staghounds will regret to hear, is temporarily indisposed, and at present unable to appear with them, but whom we all hope to see in the saddle again very shortly; Mr. Warner, of the 18th Hussars, very well mounted, whom I observed going a burster over some timber, clearing the lot in wholesale fashion; and Mr. Druce, on a big bay horse, which I noticed taking a stile in unusually good form. This specially attracted me, and riding up to this gentleman, lifting my hat, I said: "I have not the pleasure of your acquaintance, though I have that of your horse, having ridden him with the Quorn in a clipper from Gartree Hill, when necessity compelled me to charge—much against my inclination—a tall, stiff, newly-erected flight of posts and rails, over which he carried me like a bird." When the Earl of Lonsdale gave up the Cottesmore hounds, he, I was told, presented this nag to Cannon, from whom Mr. Druce obtained him—a singular piece of good luck, as a better horse I never rode. Mr. and Miss Cave, Mr. Dearle, Mr. Forster, Mr. Stollery, on his clever jumper, the well-known gray that he has ridden for the last four or five years, and many others were also there. As soon as the convivial proceedings were concluded the hounds moved off, drawing first a large field newly turned up; next a piece of osiers, then a turnip-field, when up jumped a merry brown hare, which went away a clinker. Then an opportunity was afforded of testing the speed of this pretty pack, for though mounted on an Irish horse with a turn of speed and well up to my weight, I had to stretch him a few to keep alongside of them during the fifteen minutes they raced after puss. Pressed hard, she took to a piece of covert, and though a fresh hare jumped up in view the hounds were not to be balked of their prey, and soon put an end to number one. This was a very pretty piece of sport, the hounds doing their work admirably throughout this pleasant little spurt. So far the fences were light and easily negotiable; but as we approached the Thames in the vicinity of Magna Charta Island, and also in the direction of Horton, they assumed larger proportions, bringing several well-mounted men muchly to grief. Little time elapsed before we found another hare, which we hustled away at a racing pace, running into her in some seventeen minutes or thereabouts. Having been thus far successful, we speedily were on the line of another and, this time, a stouter hare, which took us across a park-like piece of pasture-land, and over a large section of ploughed ground; then doubling back she went across some meadows in the direction of Horton. At this point she crossed a wide and deep brook—a piece of water that was big enough to stop every bold rider save one, and that one a lady, for Miss Harvey, pulling her horse together, rode fearlessly at the big jump; but her nag, hesitating for a moment on the brink of the dark and dirty-looking stream, and being compelled by its plucky rider to yield to her soft persuasions in the shape of a well-applied cut of her whip, jumped the lot, reaching the treacherous, boggy bank on the opposite side only to fall back into the middle of the brook, from which, whilst never losing her seat or her nerve, she had to be lifted off her horse by one or two gentlemen, who went breast deep in the stream, and bore her safely and unconcernedly to dry land. Whilst a portion of the field were using their best exertions to extricate the horse from his perilous position, the hounds had run into their third hare, after half-an-hour's excellent sport. Again we tried for another, and in full view of the pack up jumped a big brown hare, which went away merrily at a stunning pace. Two or three big fences winnowed the field, more than one or two biting the dust or the mud, as the case might be, and many shirking the big places or hesitating for awhile, until the hounds and the forward riders had reached the railway, when puss doubled back, making for Horton, where she was lost. After this, Mr. Scott suggested that as the field had tailed off considerably, and Sir Robert Harvey had expressed his opinion that the day was still young, the hounds should draw again for yet another hare. Thinking that as I should have to ride some eight or nine miles to Twickenham, and feeling a certain indescribable yearning for another "go in" at Mr. Stollery's ribs of beef, I quitted the gay and festive throng, and wended my way homewards after playing a capital game of knife and fork. Then reaching Twickenham in time to try a marvellously good-looking horse by driving him from Mr. Sherley's stables to the station in the dark gloom of the evening, I reached home after being on horseback for eight hours, well satisfied with such an unusually good day's sport.

CHAPTER XV.

THE ROYAL BUCKHOUNDS.

YESTERDAY being Easter Monday, the customary large concourse of holiday folks assembled at Maidenhead Thicket, in order to be present at the "meet" of the Royal Buckhounds, and to witness the uncarting of the stag. The proceedings on these festive occasions are not restrained by any of the rules usually followed in pursuing this branch of sport, the pedestrians taking for the nonce the place of the hounds; the stag, when emerging from the van, being received with shouts of uproarious delight, and pursued by the multitude until he contrives to make his way through the brushwood and takes to the open country, soon, however, leaving that portion of his pursuers behind. The royal huntsman carefully threads his way, and, by judiciously adopting a circuitous route, is enabled to save his hounds from the danger attendant upon the rush of those on horseback and in vehicles who play the second part in the chase, pursuing, as long as they are able, the flying quarry, and when it has successfully shown them a clean pair of heels, then Goodall lays on his hounds, and a more or less good run results, according to circumstances. Sometimes the stag is so bewildered by the shouts of the populace and badgered by his eager pursuers that he takes to the road, and speedily makes for a place of refuge; at other times he, by a bold course, quickly emerges from the mob that surrounds him, gains the open, and goes away a clinker. Then may be witnessed a mad stampede for awhile, many biting the dust in their inexperienced attempts to exhibit their skill in horsemanship; but rapidly "the field" is winnowed, the unaccustomed are left behind, not a few coming to grief, for

> Yonder a steed is rolled up with his master,
> Here in a double another lies cast;
> Faster and faster come grief and disaster,
> All but the good ones are weeded at last—

to quote one of Whyte-Melville's best hunting-songs. It is then that the select few who really can ride to hounds in proper form are left to the enjoyment of a rattling run, not unfrequently on these occasions going in the direction of Beaconsfield, the best line of country now left to the Royal Buckhounds. The splendid grass-fields in the vicinity of Harrow have been grievously cut up by that arch-enemy to the sports of the field, the speculative builder, who has had his wicked will, and dotted the fair lands with those hideous erections familiarly known as semi-detached villas, cunningly inserting the dangerous element of wire in the fences, so fatal to riders across country, in order to deter the knowing ones or to entrap the unwary. Leaving Windsor in good time, I trotted steadily away on Whissendine, one of Sherley's many useful nags, and with whose "pleasant leetle ways" I am well acquainted, having ridden him with much satisfaction on several occasions. Soon the towers of the grand old castle are left behind, and I pass through Eton, journeying in the direction of Bray, experiencing the feeling of exhilaration consequent upon being mounted on a pleasant horse and moving quickly through the crisp air of the early morning.

>All nature looks smiling and gay,
> So I'll join the glad throng,
> And go laughing along,
>For we'll all go a-hunting to-day—

as the old song says. Well, of all sports there can be little doubt that hunting bears off the palm; and though there is a small section of our legislators who would put an end to field-sports of every description, by destroying the game, cutting down the plantations, rooting up the gorse-covers, felling the ancient oaks and elms, levelling the beautiful hedgerows and fern-clad banks, ploughing up the deer-parks, and consequently driving the country gentlemen, thus deprived of their sports, to seek amusements in other far-off places, I do not think, looking at present prospects, that that state of things will occur in my time. It is tolerably certain that I shall not live to see "the stately halls of England," the mansions of the nobility, and the grand old historic castles shut up and dismantled, whilst the country is divided into two-acre holdings and occupied by a peasant proprietary. No, I don't think it will happen in my time; and I fancy that as long as I can ride to hounds I shall find green fields to gallop over, good covers to draw, and stout foxes to follow; and if after my time by chance this social deluge should swamp the country, I for one at any rate shall be safely landed.

Conceive anyone desiring to destroy Burnham Beeches in order to convert that hard gravelly soil into agricultural land! I remember when in a fit of economy some zealous politicians, in their burning desire to benefit the country, destroyed Hainault Forest in Essex, hewed down the ancient Fairlop Oak, and converted the once lovely glades and leafy knolls into a most hungry and capital-devouring farm. This beautiful range of woodland-wild was within six miles of Whitechapel Corner, and, if now existing, would be invaluable as one of the lungs of the vastly-increasing metropolis that is so rapidly extending in every direction. So much for economy at any price. But a truce to such discursive reflections. We bore away along quiet lanes, past many a well-kept cottage garden, richly decked with the golden crocus, the modest violet, the graceful snowdrop, and "daffodils that come before the swallows dare, and take the winds of March with beauty," by "meadows trim with daisies pied," catching every now and then a glimpse of the beautiful bends of the Thames until the high-road to the Thicket is reached, and the "fun of the fair" begins. By half-past ten Phœbus 'gan to rise, or at any rate to draw the curtains, and the larks soared to the sky. Up to this time the whole country was enveloped in mist, a sharp white frost made the fingers tingle, and the hedges were covered with rime. The thrush, rejoicing in the brightness of the day, now commenced pouring forth a song of thanksgiving from the budding branch of the old elm-tree, believing that at last the dreary winter is over, and that there is a reasonable hope of sunshine and warm weather. The wild violets and fresh primroses peep out amidst the dead leaves on the banks of the fences, the aconite is in full bloom, and the hedgerows are ready to burst forth the instant they are assured that there will be no more frost. In fact, the country is only awaiting the proverbial warm April showers to bring forth a profusion of wild blooms. Then the Thicket is reached after a smart trot of eight miles, and the scene on arrival is curious. From two to three thousand holiday folks on foot, and in every conceivable vehicle, as well as a host of horsemen on good, bad, and indifferent nags, are assembled. Around the deer-cart stands a dense mass of foot-people, anxiously awaiting the enlargement of the stag who is to provide sport on this occasion. Stalls abound for the sale of sweets, juicy oranges, cakes, and at the public-houses runs an unceasing flow of ale; and, to complete the picture, and delight the multitude, the Twyford brass band discourse music more or less sweet, adding to the originality of the proceeding, for in my long experience in hunting the music has hitherto been confined to the horn of the huntsman and the cry of the hounds. All was mirth, jollity, and good-temper.

Whilst waiting for the uncarting of the stag, I had time to look around and notice some of the *habitués* of the "Queen's," amongst whom were Lady Julia Follett, Lady Herbert, Miss Ellis, Miss Pigott, Mr. Crichell, Mr. Bowen May and his two sons, Mr. Nevill, Mr. Sherley and his son Walter—who is a chip of the old block, and bids fair to be as good a man across country as his father, for I observed him put his horse at a stiff flight of posts and rails, and afterwards at a tall fence, with much skill, pluck, and judgment—and Mr. Wise, jun. Amidst such a host it was difficult to single out even these few. Captain Hargreaves' drag, with a full load of passengers, was brought up near the starting-point, and a barouche, with four spicy bay, blood-like horses; as well as many carriages containing residents in the vicinity. By noon the fog had entirely cleared away, and the sky was cloudless, the sun shining with a brilliancy worthy of olden times. Sol, in fact, after his long seclusion, came out strong—hot and strong, I may say —and as for the peck of March dust, bushels could have been easily gathered: I took away more than I cared to carry. Now Goodall appears on the scene with Bartlett and his other whips, and thirteen and a half couples of fine hounds. It was a difficult task to pilot them through the surging crowd, but this was accomplished satisfactorily. Then the order was given for the uncarting of the deer, the doors were opened, and out bounded Express—one of the largest, Goodall told me, he had ever seen. The crowd were wedged tightly in, and no space was allowed for his passage; however, he took the matter in his own hands and cleared a way for himself, knocking down the people like ninepins, and making for the fields. After him followed scores of impetuous horsemen. What mattered it that the hounds were not even laid on, and would not be for fifteen minutes—the usual law allowed? Away they went, helter skelter, and were soon lost to sight. Then Goodall brings up the pack; they are laid on the scent, which, in consequence of the dry weather, was very indifferent, the fallow fields being as hard as the turnpike-road, and quite as dusty. At length they get away, followed by at least five hundred horsemen. At the first fence down goes one, and the brown horse is up first, and gallops wildly away. At the second another rash rider comes to sorrow. "Yoi, over!" I cried, as I saw him putting his horse at the fence in front of me, and " Yoi, over!" it was—right over, in fact—and the gray was first to find his feet, and go away at a clinking rate after the hounds. From this gentleman's acrobatic performance, I should imagine he intends to compete with the Hanlon brothers; his prospects may be said to be encouraging should he carry out his presumed intentions. With repeated checks, constant over-riding of hounds, and now and again a brisk gallop, we go in the direction of Wargrave. When this point was reached, it was found that Express had crossed the river, and the hounds came to a check. Here the bulk of the "field" stopped, as the prospect of a four-mile trot to Henley Bridge, along a dusty road, was not likely to be very enjoyable. The run may be said to have been over; but nevertheless Goodall crossed the bridge, and seemed determined to take the deer. Having seventeen miles to ride in order to catch the train, I somewhat unwillingly bent my steps homewards, for Whissendine was still as fresh as paint, carrying me over every fence that came in his way in a manner to delight anyone who loves a good mount. For an Easter hunt, the sport was fair enough; much cannot be expected where such an enormous concourse assembles. It is, in fact, a holiday giving immense pleasure to the crowd; and as the regular riders with the Royal Buckhounds have all the rest of the season to themselves, it is well that the general public should participate, once a year, in the enjoyable sport of hunting the stag. The day until sunset was lovely in the extreme; every road was thronged with pleasure-seekers, many of whom picnicked on the grass, and seemed to enjoy their outing immensely.

CHAPTER XVI.

A DAY'S COURSING.

As for coursing, I see no pleasure in it;
Dull for an hour and mad for a minute—

Was the burthen of an old, old song, expressing the opinion of one whose ardour for the chase led him to look contemptuously on the pleasures of the leash. There is coursing and coursing, I admit, and I should no more think of attending a meeting where trapped hares were the game, than I should of joining in a sparrow-match at The Pig and Whistle, to shoot for the prize of a fat pig. But, given a fine day at the end of February, when hares are sure to run stoutly, a wide tract of open country, some fine-drawn, high-bred greyhounds, a pleasant party, and a hearty welcome from the occupier of the soil, then I am quite content to make one of the throng. Never having visited this part of Kent before, I was naturally desirous of ascertaining some particulars of the locality in which I was to enjoy a day's coursing. Referring to one of Camden's ponderous volumes, I read that " Rumney Marsh ys from Limmenhill upwards a X miles in bredeth. It is a marvellous rank ground for fedying of catel by reason that the grass groweth so plentifully. It is 10 miles from east to west, and four from north to south, containing four districts, the total acreage being 46,691 acres. The lands differ in fertility; few oxen but many sheep; on an average 3 to an acre. The lands let for 20s. per acre, besides which the tenant pays 5s. in the £ for keeping up banks, roads, &c." Such was the account of Romney Marsh given by the historian writing about the date of 1580.

Starting from Cannon Street, and journeying by the South-Eastern Railway, I could not fail to be struck with the daily-increasing extension of the metropolis. Already it has reached Lewisham, once a quiet, pleasant, suburban retreat, but now linked to London by one almost continuous street. Soon every green field in this locality will be improved off the face of the earth by the speculative builder, who has his wicked will, and still stretches out his greedy arms for more land upon which to run up with haste his semi-detached villas. Then the pretty and increasing hamlet of Chiselhurst is reached, and dashing through the tunnels we fly past Sevenoaks, take a peep at Tunbridge and the hop-growing district about Marden, past Headcorn, until Ashford is reached, where I was to join the party of sportsmen bent on pursuing the "nut-brown hare" over the big fallows and the large grass-lands of Romney Marsh. On my arrival I was met by Mr. Sidney Wilmot, chairman of the Tunbridge Wells Farmers' Club, to whom I was indebted for the invitation to join in this day's sport, who had requisitioned carriages and horses from the well-known Saracen's Head, sufficient to convey the whole party to the appointed place—a distance of thirteen miles—where the day's amusement was to commence. Amongst the party assembled at the station was the ever-popular Marquess of Abergavenny, accompanied by Sir Edmund Filmer, M.P., Mr. A. Akers Douglas, M.P., Mr. E. B. Smith (Mayor of Maidstone), who, relinquishing for a few hours his arduous duties, seemed to enjoy his temporary freedom from official cares; Mr. W. H. Hodgkin, of Tunbridge Wells, whom I remember following over a big fence which brought me to grief whilst hunting with the West Kent; Messrs. H. D. Montagu Williams, Bertram Noakes, Walter Bashford, Ranking, Spencer, Pain, and the jovial secretary of the Tunbridge Wells division of the West Kent Hounds, Mr. Edward Durrant, who is to be found at every pleasant gathering or festive entertainment throughout the whole county of Kent. Asked to take a seat in a well-appointed wagonette, to which were harnessed four good-looking horses, I soon found I had joined a lively party, who beguiled the time by recounting racy anecdotes of things in general and sporting in particular, as we trotted merrily along through the quiet little villages, with their old-fashioned, thatch-covered, ivy-clad cottages and neatly-kept little gardens, where

> Fair-handed Spring unbosoms every grace;
> Throws out the snowdrop and the crocus first;
> The daisy, primrose, violet darkly blue:
> The yellow wall-flower, stained with iron brown,
> And lavish stock that scents the garden round.

The marvellously mild season having developed this floral display at an unusually early period, cowslips already having been gathered in this locality, whilst every bank in places was literally carpeted with primroses. After a brisk drive the marsh appears in sight, a wide expanse of open land, without a bush or tree, with the numerous martello towers, which were intended to keep guard over Dungeness Bay; but now that it is proposed to insidiously undermine the "silver streak," their occupation will be gone, an easy approach for continental armies, as some people think, being provided by the proposed Channel Tunnel. Pulling up at a small village, having a somewhat large and venerable church, which appeared out of proportion to the population—a public-house, grocer's shop, and a few small tenements, comprising the whole of this exceedingly small and truly rural hamlet—we were welcomed by Mr. Jones, a thorough sportsman and bold rider, who, I was told, occupied fifteen thousand acres of grass and arable land, over some of which we were to walk, for riding was, if not impossible, scarcely desirable, as the big ditches, full of mud and stagnant water, cause it to be a line of country fair to look upon but difficult to cross, though I am told that Mr. Jones followed the East Kent Hounds in a capital run over the marsh a few days since in proper form; but then he knows every inch of the country, without which knowledge the boldest rider would be bound to come to grief. Then I note some five or six brace of good-looking greyhounds, including Mr. Ralp's Gipsy, which was matched against Mr. Ovenden's Goodboy, Mr. Ovenden's Gaylad against Mr. Sampson's Zulu, Mr. Rimmer's Seabrook against Mr. Jones's Sweet Songster, Mr. Jones's Spanker against Mr. Philpot's Valley, Mr. Jones's High Chancellor against Mr. Samuel's Daniel, and two clever-looking puppies belonging to Mr. Pain and Mr. Wilmot, who were to have a trial of speed and endurance after one of the stout hares which are found in the marsh. Now a large fallow field is tried, and after traversing a considerable extent of promising land without hearing the welcome cry of "See-ho!" we see a stout old hare going away at a tremendous pace before the greyhounds could get a view of her; and it was not long before she put several fields between herself and her intending pursuers. Then we cross the road, and walk over a large tract of pasture-land; and in a few minutes we hear the cry of "See-ho!" proclaiming that a hare is found. Gipsy and Goodboy are straining in the leash, eager and ready for the chase. The hare is started, the greyhounds are quickly slipped, and away they go at a terrific pace. Sometimes Gipsy has the best of it, then Goodboy comes to the fore, then puss is hardly pressed; and, whilst going at her utmost speed, she doubles back cleverly, and both dogs overshoot her. By this clever manœuvre a temporary advantage is gained, but soon the distance between the pursued and her eager pursuers is lessened. They again come within a few feet of her. Then, following the same course, she doubles cleverly, and this time gains a considerable advantage, as I see her scuttling along at so great a speed that the betting was in favour of her. Clever as were her doubles and terrific her speed, yet she could not shake off her eager pursuers, who, stretching out literally *ventre à terre*, and using every exertion, gain on her by degrees, and finally run into her, after a severe course. During this exciting course we "were mad for a minute," though it must be admitted that in this class of sporting it is rather a dull time whilst waiting for a hare to be found. So far, therefore, I admit the burthen of the song to be correct; though those who breed greyhounds and constantly follow the sport become as ardent in pursuit of it as others are in the case of the fox. One course is very like another, the same speed and wily tact upon the part of the hare, and the same exertion and hard striving on that of the greyhounds to overtake her, in which contests these stout marsh hares have, in two cases out of three, the advantage of the greyhounds.

After traversing a considerable amount of meadow and ploughed land, climbing over innumerable and awkward sets of posts and rails, crossing the wide ditches, over narrow planks temporarily laid across, which have to be got over with a step both "light and true," again we heard the cry of "See-ho!" This time it is to be a trial of the two puppies; and Mr. Wilmot's white and Mr. Pain's brindled dogs are placed in the leash. Then the hare is started, a little law is given, and the greyhounds are slipped and go at full speed; now the white dog has the best of it, then the brindle gives him the go-by; the hare seems to have the best chance, and, by doubling and availing herself of every inch of advantage, finally eludes her pursuers, and makes good her escape. These two puppies are stout-running, fast, and enduring animals, and with luck ought to grow into note. By this time we had fully earned our luncheon, and, after a long march in the fresh air, a sandwich and a glass of sherry were acceptable, or, what was even more to the taste of some, the brown crust, the rich old Stilton cheese, and the good ale that was amply provided.

Usually an abundance of hares are to be found in Romney Marsh, but on this occasion we did not have as much sport as usual; in fact, it is rather late in the season; and much of the fallow-land where puss elects to make her form, her instinct telling her that the similarity of her colour and that of the soil renders her a less conspicuous mark for the courser, has been re-ploughed or harrowed preparatory to the sowing of the seed. Taking leave of Mr. Jones and numerous fellow-sportsmen, we retraced our steps to the South-Eastern Railway, and were soon *en route* for Tunbridge Station, where our party separated, and I quite concurred with the Marquess of Abergavenny when taking leave of him, who said if it had not been a very good day's sport, yet it had been a pleasant gathering of genial and merry sportsmen. Those who take an interest in the sports of West Kent will hear with satisfaction that since the fusion of the foxhounds with the Eridge pack, hunted by Lord George Nevill, those hunting with the united pack have had excellent sport and more opportunities of enjoying it, as may be seen by the announcement, five fixtures being advertised for this week; an inducement, consequently, for those who indulge in the pleasures of the chase to make Tunbridge Wells their headquarters. Those who do so cannot fail to be pleased with it as a place of residence, and those who hunt with the West Kent will find a crack pack of hounds, plenty of foxes, and in Lord George Nevill a true sportsman, a bold rider, worthy to be associated in the management of a pack of hounds with his uncle, the Hon. Ralph Pelham Nevill, who for many years has been the Master of the West Kent Foxhounds.

CHAPTER XVII.

HUNTING IN A HURRICANE.

DESIRING to have a preliminary canter before beginning regular hunting work, I arranged for a ride through Windsor Forest last Friday. I found a fierce wind blowing and a torrent of rain falling that looked bad for those bent on forest hunting. As the morning advanced, so the severity of the storm increased, until it became a raging tempest, the like of which I have seldom seen except in a tropical land. Having made up my mind, however, for a day's sport, and being mounted on a handsome young chestnut horse, I thought on such a sturdy steed I might brave the elements. The rain fortunately ceased before I started, but as I entered the Long Walk the raging wind swayed the stately elms, tearing off enormous branches, and strewing the ground with leafy boughs to an extraordinary extent. Cantering swiftly along, I witnessed the havoc that was going on all around me, keeping as far to windward of the big bending trees as possible, and feeling a certain amount of satisfaction at running the gauntlet safely amidst the falling limbs of venerable timber, the strength of the wind increasing as time went on. Having passed undamaged through the Long Walk, I reached the open part of the park, and went sailing merrily over the grass; then away by Fern Hill until the racecourse was reached, then on by the Kennels, arriving at the Royal Hotel just after Goodall had started with the hounds and small "field" who had ventured upon a ride on this unpromising morning.

The Earl of Cork, the Master of the Buckhounds, was not present, though his son (Lord Dungarvan) put in an appearance. The hounds were trotted off to a spot contiguous to South Lodge, the residence of Sir W. Hayter, a distance of some three miles or more, where the deer Edgerly had been uncarted, and the hounds being laid on at once, went away at a rattling pace through the hurly-burly of the storm, making for Easthampstead Park, the seat of the Marquis of Downshire. All the while the wind howled and raged furiously, sturdy oaks creaked and groaned as their limbs were riven or remorselessly torn off, whilst fine beeches and other trees, the growth of many years, were torn up by the roots, one actually falling between the pack and their huntsman, fortunately without doing damage to either. Leaving Easthampstead Park behind, the hounds ran for Cæsar's Camp, then away by Gravel Hill, then on by Swinley Paddocks, through the forest, where the deer, being pressed hard, jumped the fence into Windsor Park, where he was left. The pack were soon trotted back to the kennels, with only one hound missing, notwithstanding the wildness of the weather. It was almost impossible to ride to hounds on such a day as this; neither the cry of the pack nor the shrill note of the huntsman's horn could be heard, and if you once lost sight of them there was no chance of getting to them again, consequently the "field" was scattered, many being thrown out long before the end of the run. Certainly this was an unparalleled day's sport. At one time the gale blew so hard and the hailstones fell so thick and sharp that my young horse stopped dead, until I persuaded him to persevere, though for a few minutes rather unwillingly. Evidently his nerves were affected, for when put in the stable he was looking about in an excited way instead of eating his corn. I believe horses to be very nervous animals, and that often they do things through fear that lead to their being treated as vicious creatures, instead of being kindly encouraged and gently used. Certainly hunting in a hurricane is calculated to make one rather nervous, as riding amidst the fallen branches, listening to the roar of the wind, the cracking of the timber, finding your path stopped by a huge trunk, expecting every minute that a big branch might possibly fall on as well as before you, is not calculated to inspire confidence in either man or beast. However, I had at any rate a good gallop on a good horse, and should not be deterred on another occasion from having a day's forest hunting, however angry and unpleasant the weather might be; as, after my experience of this notable gale, I cannot imagine that anything could possibly be worse than that which I experienced on this occasion. Fortunately such terrific storms are not frequent, or our stock of fine timber would be greatly reduced, for I dare not venture to state the number of large trees I saw blown down or greatly damaged throughout the whole extent both of Windsor Forest and Park.

Prior to riding with "The Queen's," I had an opportunity of going over the kennels and seeing the hounds on the flags, recognising some of my old friends—Rummager and Wizard, to wit—and I can say, without fear of contradiction, that the whole forty-seven and a half couples of Royal Buckhounds are as noble a lot of animals as ever have been seen at Ascot, at any rate within my memory, which extends beyond forty years. Frank Goodall may well be proud of this year's entries, consisting of nine and a half couples of dogs and six and a half couples of "ladies," and he may safely challenge comparison with those of any hunt in the kingdom—that is to say, if I know anything of such matters. The Belvoir blood largely predominates, no less than six couples being of that well-known strain of high-class foxhounds, from which I should select Brusher, Bellman, Bertha, Chorus, Topthorn, and Trojan as some of the finest of the lot. The Duke of Grafton's blood has also been introduced —Norman, Noble, Norah, and Novelty (by Stormer; dam, the Belvoir Needful) are first-rate specimens. Theodore and Thrifty well represent the Cottesmore kennels, being by Prodigal; dam, the Belvoir Tutoress. Of the home-bred hounds—Veteran, Vesper, Venus, and Vengeance (by General; dam, Mr. Foljambe's Violet)—it may be said that a finer lot of young hounds cannot be imagined. The wonderful attention that the royal huntsman pays to the pack under his charge must be seen to be fully appreciated. Comins, from the Hey-throp, is the new whip, and seems likely to be an acquisition, being pleasant, shrewd, and obliging, as well as master of his business. Having formed, after close inspection, such a favourable opinion of the condition of the hounds, I thought it advisable to avail myself of the permission I had received to inspect the royal stud of hunters provided for Goodall and his merry men "when a hunting they do go," now that winter is approaching, that pleasant time of year—

> When hill and dale and woodland shall joyously resound
> With the huntsman's cheery halloo and the music of the hound.

The stable in which the stud is located is at Cumberland Lodge, about three miles from the kennels, in a lovely part of Windsor Park. Driving from Ascot Heath on a bright autumn day, such as that which preceded the hurricane, all nature seemed smiling and gay indeed. Innumerable rabbits cropped the abundant herbage, or raced after each other in and out of the dense mass of ferns. Gorgeous pheasants sunned themselves in the bright rays, hardly caring to rise at our approach, and even then only lazily flying a few yards. Herds of fallow-deer and fawns were quietly feeding around us, whilst the occasional hoarse bellow of the red-deer was heard in the distance, sending an angry defiance to his fellow stags; this being the season at which he is somewhat quarrelsome and dangerous, as notified on the placards suspended on trees adjacent to the thoroughfares. It is impossible to describe the beauty of the foliage, alas! so soon to be literally blown to the winds. Owing to the early frosts which prevailed, the more sensitive trees assumed the most lovely hues, the Spanish chestnuts, horse chestnuts, and limes being specially noticeable for their brilliant colours, seen amidst the still deep green of the oaks and elms, standing as they did intermingled with each other in this grand and widely-extending historic old Park. On my arrival at Cumberland Lodge I met Mr. Miles, who for the last thirty-eight years has resided at this pleasant abode, having charge of the stud, numbering this year some twenty in all. Upon entering the stables one is struck with the solidity and height of the buildings, showing that they were built long prior to the cement or compo era—fit to stand against the fiercest blasts or the ravages of years. Spacious, well drained and ventilated, and kept in the most perfect order, they will be found in all probability standing when the modern quickly-run-up, lightly-timbered, brick-and-a-half contract edifices are crumbled into dust.

The huntsman and whips are, I should say, likely to be better carried than they have been for some years past, Lord Cork having selected some right good ones, which, under the special and attentive care of Mr. Miles, look as fit as the proverbial fiddles, and I should say that in the hands of workmen such a string of quality should run to a very pretty tune. Crusader, a fine gray horse about seventeen hands high, is a rare specimen of a high-class hunter. Those who attended the Ascot meeting will probably remember Crusader, who carried in grand form the noble Master of the Buckhounds in the royal procession on the Cup-day. Since the days of Charles Davis's favourite, Hermit, I should say no better nag has been seen within the walls of Cumberland Lodge. High-bred, with deep girth, rare shoulders, good short flat legs, muscular thighs, an intelligent head, and a good temper—I do not know what else is required to constitute a real hunter, excepting, of course, speed, and the knowledge of how to negotiate big fences, brawling brooks, and cramped places—qualities which I am told he possesses in the highest degree. Norman, a chestnut horse, is another of Goodall's favourites, and is a handsome, gentle, well-mannered nag, thoroughly up to his business. Conjurer and Comet are two useful-looking horses, seeming likely to be found in the front rank, after a rattling gallop, if inquired for at the finish.

I think I shall not be far wrong if I predict a good time for both huntsmen and whips during the coming season. With unsafe, irritable, awkward horses, the attention which should be paid to the hounds is expended in controlling a wayward, ill-conditioned brute, going with his head up in the air, and requiring skilful guiding; so that the servant, be he huntsman or whip, has no chance of performing his duty in a satisfactory way. It is too much the fashion, I think, to deem any horse good enough to carry a whip. A great mistake, indeed, in my opinion. A good fencer, even if slightly troubled with "the slows," I should prefer to a rushing, eager, over-jumping brute, with a mouth as hard as a blacksmith's anvil; but perhaps I am particular. Mr. Miles was good enough to show us the grandest vine in the world, one that dwarfs that of Hampton Court to insignificant proportions, extending, as does the Cumberland Lodge vine, over a space of 150 feet, or, to be precise, 160 feet, which is, I believe, the exact measurement. The product of this vine is very great, being computed by the ton, the sort being the black Hamburg. The schools initiated by the late Prince Consort were next pointed out. Every *employé*, be his rank what it may, enjoys the privilege of having his children educated and partly clothed by the benevolent consideration of that kindly-hearted and generous Prince, who is spoken of with the deepest respect. A happy community is that around Cumberland Lodge, numbering in all some one hundred and fifty, and it would appear that her Royal Highness Princess Christian, aided by her husband, follows the traditions of her father in her care of those, however humble they may be, who as labourers or servants on the royal domain have a claim on her kindness and consideration. After thanking Mr. and Mrs. Miles for the far more than ordinary attention shown to myself and friends, which, by-the-way, was thoroughly appreciated by the lady of our party, I sought out Mr. Prince, the stud-groom to his Royal Highness the Prince of Wales, with the view of taking a cursory view of his Royal Highness's hunters. Being introduced to Colonel Nigel Kingscote, the Master of the Horse to the Prince of Wales, I was most courteously received, and had permission instantly accorded to go over the stables; not the less cordially granted, I believe, by the fact of my having attended the day's sport with the Devon and Somerset Staghounds on the occasion of the Prince's visit last year. We somewhat hurriedly passed through the beautiful stables, examining the two favourite nags that carry her Royal Highness the Princess of Wales, and the ten very high-class, heavy-weight hunters selected for the Prince's use. At this moment horses are seen at greater disadvantage than at any other period of the year; changing, as they are, their coats, they want the bloom which will be found on them a week or two hence. Nevertheless, these fine animals, which are under the charge of Mr. Prince, are in rare form, and I should say there is no crowned head in the world who can boast of such a lot of high-class horses—fit to carry a heavy weight over the stiffest country in the kingdom. After exhausting the wonders of Cumberland Lodge, a pleasant drive through a beautiful country brought us to Egham.

CHAPTER XVIII.

MELTON MOWBRAY.

WHEN Nimrod wrote in the pages of the "Quarterly Review," some half century since, in a style never excelled by any writer on matters appertaining to "the chase," he designated Melton Mowbray, "this renowned metropolis of the fox-hunting world."

Having recently revisited the scenes of past delights, with the view of galloping once more over the broad pastures of Leicestershire, I rejoice to say that the ancient "Mercat Town," as Camden described it ages ago, still maintains its supremacy, and is, as of yore, the abiding-place of those who delight in the noble sport and desire to enjoy to the fullest extent the pleasure of hunting the fox over the finest country in the world, and witnessing the performances of the three most celebrated packs of hounds—viz. the Quorn, the Belvoir, and the Cottesmore, each of which can be reached within easy distance, thus affording the opportunity of riding to hounds every day in the week.

A quieter town on a Sunday than Melton Mowbray cannot be imagined. The grand old church, the pride of the Meltonians, was well filled at the morning service; after attending which I roamed over the town to note the alterations and improvements that have been made since my last visit, dating three years back. I had no difficulty in finding out the alterations, but could not discern the improvements. Two more lines of railway, each passing through the best part of the country, have been added, and this addition is certainly not an improvement as respects riding to hounds; the other alterations take the form of a factory or two, with tall chimneys belching forth clouds of smoke, and this does not improve the rural aspect of the Metropolis of the Chase.

Falling in with Mr. Martin, stud-groom to the Earl of Wilton, who was going to the stables to see the nags done up for the night, he kindly afforded me an opportunity of passing through and examining the high-class horses in the fourteen well-lighted, thoroughly-ventilated, and admirably-kept boxes, which stand in a line and can be seen at a glance. Amongst these horses are some pictures of animals, fit to carry thirteen stone to the fastest hounds in the world, all seeming good-tempered and in capital condition, Egerton Lodge, the residence of the venerable earl who has hunted from Melton for considerably over fifty years, being in readiness for his lordship, who, by-the-way, I am happy to be able to say, is at the present time residing there with the Countess of Wilton, having Colonel Forester and Sir Henry Des Vœux as visitors. As yet Lord Wilton has not appeared in the saddle, but it is to be hoped that he will once more join in the sport in which he has so long delighted.

Having in view the fact that I was going to attend one of the best " meets " of the Quorn in the morning, and remembering the well-worn old proverb, that "Early to bed and early to rise, makes a man healthy, wealthy, and wise," I determined to give it a trial, arising in the morning decidedly healthy and fit to go, finding, as respected the wealth, and the wisdom, that things remained much as they were. On the breakfast-table I found the elaborate cards of the meets of the different packs, forwarded by Mr. Loxley and Mr. Mills, from which I learned that I had well timed my visit, as I should be able to see each of the renowned packs at their best fixtures during the week, and that, filling up my time on off-days by looking over the different studs, visiting the kennels, generally surveying the town, and partaking of the abundant hospitality of the inhabitants, of which I have had ample experience on former occasions, I should, as usual, have an exceedingly good time during my stay.

The meet on this occasion was Kirby Gate, and, the morning being fine, I mounted a good-looking gray horse, which I was told had formerly carried Sir Watkin Wynn, feeling satisfied that I should have a "safe conveyance," to use a phrase much in vogue amongst sporting people at the present time. As I rode along to cover I overtook Mr. Burbidge, driving quietly along, advancing years having compelled this fine old sportsman to relinquish the saddle and trust to wheels, though his trust proved fallacious, I am sorry to say, as, a short time since, when accompanying the hounds, his horse, doubtless an old hunter—unable to withstand the temptation to join in the chase—bolted and charged one or two gates, but fortunately without seriously injuring his master.

Arriving at Kirby Gate, I found a strong muster of

pedestrians, equestrians, and people in all sorts of vehicles, awaiting the arrival of the Quorn, showing that the sport is as popular as ever, and attracts as much, or even more attention than in bygone days. Punctual to time, Mr. Coupland, the Master of the Quorn, rode up, followed by Tom Firr and his twenty-one couple of fine hounds—ladies to-day—in brilliant, or what I should call racing, condition. Then the arrivals increase, and I have a cheery greeting from Captain Elmhirst and a welcome from the master, who I was glad to find has regained his old form. Next I see Captain Middleton, and I was glad to find him none the worse for the severe fall he had in the spring. Then I observe Mr. Lubbock mounted on a remarkably clever-looking gray, which I recollect to have seen him ride a year or two since. Then my attention is attracted by the appearance on the scene of several ladies, and I find the Countess of Cardigan well mounted. Lady Florence Dixie next arrives, looking as fit to go as ever, receiving many congratulations on her reappearance in these parts, her ladyship having been in distant countries of late, where they hunt not the fox. Then Mr. Chaplin, of Brooksby, rides up, accompanied by his daughter, on a good-looking horse, going well to hounds on all occasions. Then I notice Mr. W. Chaplin, of Wyndham Lodge, and his daughter, who, I am told, goes like a bird; Captain and Mrs. Molyneux, both of whom are difficult to beat; Mr. Parker, who is living this year at Wicklow Lodge; Captain Whitmore, of four-in-hand fame; Mr. and Mrs. Pennington (*née* Hartopp), of Dalby Hall; Miss Livingstone, who, I am told, is a first-class performer; General Burnaby, Captain Farley Turner, Sir

F. Fowke, Captain Hume, Messrs. Markham, Hare, Johnston, Cooper; Captain Goodchild, Dr. Powell, Captain Grimston, Captain Stephen, Messrs. Knowles, Pryor, Hanbury, Praed, and Beaumont; Custance, as cheerful as ever, extremely well mounted, and ready to go the pace, in the very first flight, as usual. Next I notice some of the inhabitants of Melton and the vicinity, and sundry farmers, who, in spite of their unfortunate seasons, are not to be balked of their favourite pastime, bad times notwithstanding. Amongst them I find the brothers S. and H. Black, good men and true over the grass; Messrs. Fox, Matts, Carver (a stanch preserver of foxes), Simkin, Alfred, Childs, Goodall, Saunders, Miles and brother, &c. Then a celebrity, the jovial sporting butcher of Melton, Mr. Morris, who, by no means ashamed of his calling, rides in a light blue jacket, with a bunch of choice Neapolitan violets in his button-hole, appearing to be on the best terms with everyone, riding a playful animal that I remember to have seen gamboling merrily, but, being bought by this heavy-weight eager sportsman, has met with its master at last.

Time being up, we trotted away for Gartree Hill, a noted covert and sure find. As we journeyed along, I saw Mr. Pain riding a grand four-year-old bay horse, which I learned belongs to Mr. Alfred Childs, and seems likely to make a real hunter. The instant the hounds were thrown into covert a fox broke away without a minute's delay, and we had a pleasant little scurry at a slapping pace, running him to ground in a drain in Sandy Lane, near Mr. Copley's farm, the run barely lasting a quarter of an hour. This, however, served as a breather for the nags, fitting them for a longer gallop later on. Then we trotted back to Gartree Hill, which was drawn blank, the noise of the foot-people assembled on the hill causing, no doubt, the foxes to leave the covert of that popular gorse for some quieter retreat. From thence we moved to Sir Francis Burdett's covert, where a fox was viewed going away in the direction of the Burrow Hills. Bearing to the left, he ran below the hills, making for Little Dalby, crossing the lawn of Dalby Hall at a racing pace, up to which point my gallant gray carried me first of all this large field. I do not say this in a boastful spirit by any means, but simply to point out to some of my young friends—who occasionally speak rather disrespectfully of the doings of us elderly men—that, gray hairs notwithstanding, there is life in some of the old dogs yet. From thence the fox made for the Punch Bowl Covert, running along the hillside, going for Gartree Hill, and then away to Great Dalby at a rattling pace. At one time the speed was fast and furious; there was a crash of timber, several good men went wrong, and I saw three horses running riderless. Away, until within a short distance of the new railway from Melton to Harborough, where we came to a check. Picking up the scent, the hounds then ran him in the direction of Burrow Hills; but, bearing to the right, the fox made for Sir Francis Burdett's covert again; then going once more over the hills, he made for Little Dalby, running thorugh the plantations, pointing for Melton; but the hounds getting on good terms with him, they ran into him and broke him up within a mile or so of Melton, after a capital, enjoyable run over a good country, during which I do not think I ever was off the grass.

The aspect of the country on the morning succeeding the meet at Kirby Gate was very different from the bright and glorious day when I rode with the Quorn, for the snow fell in large flakes and the cold was excessive. The day was that of the weekly market, and the town was alive with farmers and visitors bent upon buying or selling the various commodities displayed, varying from a hand-basin to a heifer; and a brisk trade was driven, notwithstanding the falling snow and the muddy state of the streets.

The fixture for the Cottesmore Hounds was Tilton Wood, eleven miles from Melton. The state of the weather and the distance to covert determined me to postpone riding with this crack pack until a more favourable opportunity. Accordingly I spent my time in looking over some of the fine studs of grand horses, attending the cattle-market, where I was greatly tempted to bid for an extremely small calf, which I really thought must be very cheap at seven shillings and sixpence; but whilst I was endeavouring to make up my mind to embark my capital in this promising venture, the auctioneer abruptly knocked it down for the trifling sum of eight shillings; and perhaps it was all for the best, for I doubt if I should have known what to do with it. Then I visited the museum, on the portal of which I read the words "Maison Dieu, 1640," and, entering into the ancient edifice, I examined the curious collection of what may be described as odds and ends; not finding, however, since my last visit to Melton, any remarkable additions to the articles under the charge of the venerable dame who accompanied me round.

K

A cheery personage was this old lady, for she told me she was as happy as a bird on the modest stipend of four shillings per week, augmented by the donations of visitors, which I should think would not greatly swell the total; but then there was a cosy little room and a brisk fire burning, and I thought she might have gone farther and fared worse. As I emerged the bells of the venerable church were chiming lustily, and I listened with pleasure to their oft-repeated inquiry of "Oh where and oh where is my Highland laddie gone?" True it is that I was only a visitor, or I might, if I lived beneath the venerable tower, find this reiteration monotonous, if not wearisome.

Four o'clock having been fixed by Mr. Hughes, the stud-groom to Mr. Behrens, for an inspection of his stud of over thirty high-class hunters, I was punctual in keeping my appointment, knowing from previous experience that a treat was in store for one who appreciated horses of this class; and, as I saw them stripped one by one, and turned to the light, so that I might note their shape and make, I could but admire the judgment of those who selected them, and the care bestowed upon them by Mr. Hughes, for it would be impossible to find any stud in finer condition or fitter to go the pace. The sires of many of these nags, some winners of steeplechases and hurdle-races, are John Davis and Brocket, both horses of renown. A pleasant feature in this large establishment is the presence of birds and animals that rove at pleasure through the stables. On that high-bred hunter two couples of handsome bantams comfortably roost, and reluctantly shift their quarters so that the clothing may be stripped to enable me to form an opinion of the shape and make of the nag. There a fine goat visits the different boxes, fraternising with the steeds, and partaking freely of the oats which are provided for the afternoon feed, whilst fox-terriers and cats live on amicable terms in this united family. This association tends, Mr. Hughes informs me, to render the horses gentle and tractable; and I went without hesitation up to the side of every one of these spirited horses, not seeing in any case a vicious-looking or ill-tempered animal; and the conclusion I have long since arrived at was confirmed, that kindness and confidence, combined with gentle treatment, will have more effect on the tempers of animals than any amount of rough treatment or undue and excessive punishment. As I walked back to my hotel I met several well-mounted men returning from the chase, and heard that the Cottesmore had had a fair day's sport, notwithstanding the inclemency of the weather.

On the following day the Belvoir Hounds, I found, would meet at Waltham, about five miles from Melton, and I was told that the first covert that would be drawn was the gorse known as Burbidge's Cover, within two miles of Melton. Thither several sportsmen repaired, but as I wished to see the Duke of Rutland's beautiful pack, and mistrusted common report, I cantered over to the "meet," the morning being fine, though the weather was cold and the snow still lay in sheltered places. A moderate "field" only assembled at Langham, and I had time to examine this crack lot of hounds, and after looking over them, noting their evenness, fine condition, and uniformity of colour, I saw no reason to alter an opinion expressed some four years back when asked which of the three celebrated packs I considered the best. "The Belvoir for beauty, the Cottesmore for quality, and the Quorn for speed," was my reply; and I think those who ride with these packs will acknowledge that I am not far out in my judgment. Frank Gillard, the persevering huntsman of the Belvoir, and his whips seemed to be very well mounted, and in good fettle to show sport over the fine country hunted by the Duke of Rutland in the liberal way which he has for so many years pursued, maintaining a noble pack and large establishment for the amusement of others rather than his own enjoyment. The word being given, we trotted off for Burbidge's Cover, meeting many knowing folks on the road, who had saved a mile or two by not going to the "meet." Then the Countess Grey de Wilton, a very well-known and graceful performer over the pastures of Leicestershire, drives up. Then I notice Mr. B. W. Lubbock, well mounted as usual; Mr. Parker, on a very good-looking, well-bred chestnut; Captain Ashton, of Burton Hall, a newly-built mansion and stables, placed in the heart of the country about three miles from Melton; Captain and Hon. Mrs. Molineux; Mr. and Mrs. Money Wigram; Captain Middleton, on a fine fencer; Mr. and Mrs. Pennington; Mr. Pryor; Mr. Baldock; Captain Elmhirst, pleasant and agreeable as usual; Mr. Alfred Childs; Major Longstaffe; Mr. Algernon Turnor, etc.

In attendance at the coverside was the veteran and greatly-respected owner, Mr. Burbidge, in a carriage, being no longer to be found in the first flight as in days of yore; and greatly must the heart of this fine old sportsman have been rejoiced at the first draw of the season of his new covert on the bank of the River Eye, for no sooner were the hounds halloed in than several foxes were on foot, one breaking away and going in the direction of a good line of country; but, his heart failing him, he doubled back, and regained the shelter of the gorse. The hounds in the meanwhile were not idle, and four brace of foxes were on foot at the same time, one, I believe, being chopped by the hounds, and the others rattled about the covert. Then "Tally ho, tally ho!" is heard, for a fox has gone away, crossing the Eye, and is seen racing at a rattling pace in the direction of Brentingby. The crossing of the river is the first difficulty to be encountered, the banks are very steep, and the ford, though not deep, is stony, and is not altogether a place I should cross for choice on a fresh, young, eager horse. Getting over this obstacle without difficulty, I found the grass rode beautifully. Having seen the fox when he broke covert, I thought it was probable he would lead us a lively dance, as he seemed a varmint sort of animal, and I pushed the little horse upon which I had elected to ride along the green pastures at a rattling pace. A slight check then occurred, but Gillard making a rapid cast, the hounds quickly picked up the scent, and went away again at a merry pace, making for Sapcote Lodge. Then I see a fine line of country before me, the hounds stooping well to the scent in eager pursuit of a stout fox, and it looks as if we are in for a good run. There is no time for craning, an ugly-looking fence has to be got over; two or three hard-riding men charge it, and land safely. Knowing full well if I shirked it I should be out of the hunt altogether, I sent the nag at it with a will; but not being up to my weight, he jumps a trifle short, and we come down a regular cropper, there being a big ditch on the farther side which neither of us bargained for. However, you cannot have omelets without the breaking of eggs, and you cannot ride to hounds without coming occasionally to grief.

"I was very nearly jumping on you," said Captain Molineux; "but I pulled up my horse just in time."

Thanking him for his kind consideration—as otherwise the matter might have become somewhat complicated—I mounted, and resumed the chase, the hounds running in a direct line for Caxton's Covert, being close to the fox's brush as they raced up the hillside. Then he crosses Stapleford Park, and there is some slight delay, the gate being locked. The difficulty, however, is speedily overcome. In the meantime the hounds are running hard through the College plantation, driving Reynard out of the park, pressing him so closely that he sought safety in a drain. Here he was not allowed to remain. A terrier being sent in after him, he bolted out, and I thought from his appearance he meant giving us another spin; but, after running a short ring, he again went to ground. Being, however, scared from his hiding-place by the agency of a lighted squib, he bolted once more, and was speedily run into and broken up, Frank Gillard blooding the young hounds, amidst loud cries of "Who-hoop, who-hoop!" and presenting the brush to Mr. Robert Wright. This was a pleasant scurry, mostly over a fair line of country, until Stapleford Park was reached. At this point there is a line of railway and a canal, and unless you know your way about, you are apt to get a little mixed up and lose your place. The hounds were then trotted away for Freeby Wood, Gillard trying to find an outlying fox in the vicinity of Saxby. Not succeeding, however, the hounds were thrown into Freeby Wood, and a fox was promptly on foot, and, after being rattled about the covert for awhile, he breaks away, making for Waltham Thorns, running through that covert, and going in the direction of Waltham village. Then crossing over the Melton road, the hounds go at a swingeing pace over the grass, crossing the brook, a nasty place, likely to bring one to grief; then away over the railway to Goadby Gorse, thence on to Bullimore, where the hounds were at fault, and we lost our fox after a fair run over a good country. Amongst those going in the first flight were Mr. B. W. Lubbock, Captain Elmhirst, and Captain Middleton, with many others who are usually found in a good place.

As I rode home, thoroughly satisfied with the day's sport, I felt fully impressed with the words of a favourite old hunting-song:

>   There is only one cure for all maladies sure,
>   That reacheth the heart to its core;
>   'Tis the sound of the horn, on a fine hunting morn,
>   And where is the heart wishing more?

CHAPTER XIX.

HUNTING AT BRIGHTON.

> The autumn fast is waning,
>   The air is brisk and clear,
> For winter is approaching,
>   That pleasant time of year;
> When hill, and dale, and woodland shall joyously resound
> With the huntsman's cheery halloo and the music of the hound.

THE hunting at the favourite seaside resort—Brighton as we call it nowadays, but known as Brighthelmstone in the good old times when George the Fourth was king—commenced with unusual *éclat* and great success. This city by the sea is overflowing with visitors, many of whom are attracted by the opportunities of enjoying thoroughly good sport over the breezy downs in the vicinity of this pleasantest of all watering-places. First and foremost, they can ride with the well-known and thoroughly sporting pack, the Southdown Foxhounds, which, over hill and dale and through the woodland wild, will lead you as merry a dance as you can desire. Those who wish to enjoy a thoroughly good day's sport can always insure it if they follow in the wake of Champion and his well-bred lot of first-class hounds. This persevering huntsman has carried the horn for the last twenty-two or twenty-three years, and being well supported by the popular Master of the Southdown (Mr. Streatfield), never fails to show a good run if it is possible to do so. The landowners and tenant-farmers have the most liberal views in regard to fox-hunting, not deigning to look at a piece of well-trampled wheat, but preserving foxes, and encouraging this the noblest of all our national sports. If the visitor to this fashionable resort should prefer riding with harriers, he has the chance of two of the best packs in England. First, if he is a real lover of hunting—one who delights to see a pack of true-bred harriers puzzle out the line of a sturdy hare over the bold and open downs which form their country—then he should ride with Mr. Steyning Beard's celebrated pack, the Brookside; or if he should prefer a clinking good gallop for twenty-five minutes, then he should choose the Brighton Harriers, when Mr. Dewe will give him the opportunity of galloping his hardest, for this pack are racers, every hound being a draft from some well-known kennel of foxhounds, being entered to hare, and invariably showing good sport, which they could not do unless they were speedy, as the large "fields" which ride with this popular pack are difficult to hold in hand, necessitating prompt action on the part of the huntsman to get away from the crowd and give the hounds a fair chance. Once let them draw clear from the large "field," and it will be a good man who lives alongside of, much less rides over, Mr. Dewe's beauties.

The first meet of the season of the Southdown took place at the kennels at Ringmer, when some one hundred and forty well-mounted men and ten or twelve ladies assembled, amongst whom were many well-known performers. First and foremost amongst the arrivals was Mr. Streatfield, the popular master, to whose persevering efforts much of the success of this crack hunt is due; Lord Gage (of Firle); the Earl of Lewes (a nailer across a stiff country); Lord Henry Nevill (a bad man to follow if your heart is not in the right place); Major-Gen. Hepburn, Major Shifner, Capt. Brand, Mr. A. Brand and Mr. C. Brand (from Glynde), Mr. Ingram (of Chailey), Mr. W. H. Hodgson (from Tunbridge Wells), Mr. Slater, jun. (Newick Park), Mr. Campion (of Danny Park), Captain Buckle, Mr. Philcox, Mr. and Mrs. Dewe, Mr. Broadwood, the Messrs. Kennedy, Mr. A. Dupont, Mr. Maule, and a host of others, who, from want of space, I am unable to particularise. It will be seen from the foregoing list that the South Down pack does not lack influential supporters. After an elegant breakfast, which is the custom, and a very pleasant one too, of this hunt, Champion sounded his horn, and proceeded to open the business of the season. Sixteen couples of blooming hounds formed the pack, which was accompanied by Harry Parker, the first, and Charles Kennet, the second whip. Proceeding to Glyndbourne, they drew The Mound without finding, but arriving at Glynde Holt they were soon on the line of an old fox, who was disinclined to leave the covert, but being forced at last to fly, plucked up courage and went away over the open country in view of most of the field. "Gone away! Gone away!" was the cry, and away across the grass we went at a rattling pace, making for Glyndbourne; but leaving that covert the fox made for the Roughs, where he dwelt for some time, and not having the pluck to face the open again he was run into and speedily broken up. A second fox was found at Black Shaw Copse, which showed the field a fair hunting run, being finally pulled down at a covert near Firle. Thus auspiciously was the season commenced. On the 7th the meet of these hounds was Buckingham Manor House, near Shoreham, the residence of Mr. J. H. Bridger, a staunch supporter of the noble sport, and a wonderful preserver of foxes. Here in a paddock, in front of the house, a large company was visible, on horseback, in carriages and on foot. A *recherché* breakfast was provided, after which Champion proceeded to draw for a fox in a piece of rape on a hillside near at hand. But a very short time elapsed ere the "hill and dale and woodland re-echoed back the sound of the halloo of the huntsman and the music of the hound." Sharp, short, and decisive was this spurt; for coursing the cub at a racing pace for some fifteen minutes, he was run into and broken up, after a very brief career. So abundant were the foxes in this sporting locality that another being found in a piece of rape, and being unable to escape from the bloodthirsty hounds, he too was numbered amongst the slain. After this another was viewed going in the direction of Thunder's Barrow, and the hounds being promptly laid on his line, he made for the Tenantry Gorse, but fearing to tarry there he tried the Roughs, which were soon made too hot to hold him, and he slipped through the Beeding Gorse, making for Erringham, where he ran into a piece of gorse; but thinking it unadvisable to remain long in the shelter of the covert, he bolted, in view, with the pack close at his heels. He eventually contrived, although several of the leading hounds were within a few yards of his brush, to outpace them, and gave them the slip in Beeding Shaw. It will be seen by the foregoing account that the prospects of the Southdown are most promising. Foxes abound, the hounds are as fit to go as they can possibly be, and Champion is as energetic and persevering as ever. The Brookside have been showing some good sport. Hares are abundant, and a visit to this beautiful pack of old-fashioned harriers will well repay the trouble. The kennels are situated near Rottingdean, close adjacent to the residence of Mr. Steyning Beard, the present master. These well-known hounds have been in the possession of the family during the whole of the present century, invariably showing good sport; which is easily accounted for when it is explained that the master hunts them himself, and allows the hounds to pick out the line of the hare themselves, which they do most musically and with the greatest diligence. This is real hare-hunting, where the hounds are allowed to do the work unaided, and the result shows the soundness of the policy, for I have seen some of the best runs that I ever enjoyed with any harriers amongst the many I have ridden with in my time. The fixture on the 4th was Harvey Cross, a mile or two from Rottingdean, on which occasion the pack had two excellent runs. The first hare was found by a shepherd on Middle Brow, and at the welcome sound of "So-ho!" the pack were soon brought to the halloa, when up started puss, who led them a merry chase up and down the steep hills—which, by-the-way, it takes some nerve to negotiate—finally being killed in Kingston Furze, after a clinking run of two hours and a half. A second hare was put up on Swanboro' Combe, which went down the steep descent at a terrific pace, and raced over the beautiful downs for a full hour, being finally run into and killed. This was a glorious but not unusual specimen of the sport which Mr. Steyning Beard shows to those who ride with the Brookside.

On Saturday last the Brighton Harriers met at Southwick Common, and arriving at the appointed place, Sherwood was to be seen with sixteen-and-a-half couples of hounds in fine form. Very well horsed was this clever huntsman, who carries the horn now in place of Mr. Dewe, who, in consequence of a fall at the close of the last season, is not quite up to the mark at present. Owing to there being a near meet of the Southdown the field was far smaller than usual, numbering from fifty to sixty only. An old adage, however, may be applied to the absentees, viz. "that their room was better than their company." I mean only in respect to sport, for very large fields are not conducive to it. The master was present on wheels, and many amongst the regular riders with this pack, well mounted and hard to beat over the steep downs. At a signal from Mr. Dewe, Sherwood proceeded to draw for a hare in a piece of rape close to the Windmill, when in an instant up jumped puss and ran, at a slapping pace, straight for Mannington's training-stables, then doubling back she crossed the Shoreham Road, bending to the right, and running over Thunder's Barrow, over Cock-a-Roost Hill, the hounds bustling her so hard that she sought refuge in the well-known fox covert, Tenantry Furze, where they left her. This was a pleasant run. The scent however was indifferent, or this stout-running hare would not have so readily escaped, as when the hounds were able to get on good terms with her they went the pace, streaming up an exceedingly steep hill, followed only by one or two daring riders.

Returning to the same piece of rape, a second hare was speedily found, which crossed over the Shoreham Road and ran along the valley to Kingston village, up to Buckenham, and away over Thunder's Barrow to Portslade, and thence to Mr. Gardner's, where the hounds viewed her and speedily ran into her after an excellent burst. It will be seen by the foregoing account that there is no lack of sport with either of these noted packs. To me there is something particularly pleasing in galloping on a clever steed over the open downs. Brighton, being within such an easy journey of the metropolis, offers many inducements for those who wish to enjoy a few days' sport, and who, from circumstances, cannot spare time to travel as far as Melton, Market Harborough, or Rugby. Those who do not bring their own horses will find a stud of from eighty to one hundred at Mr. Dupont's establishment, the West Brighton Riding-school, amongst which they will be hard to suit who cannot select some to please. As the horses of this stud are generally in demand, it is advisable to make arrangements in advance.

CHAPTER XX.

CUB-HUNTING.

IN all hunting centres the note of preparation is being sounded for the coming season, which commences on the first day of November. Already the Royal Buckhounds have been out in the forest, with the view of blooding the pack. The first meet was at Ascot, the deer being uncarted at Swinley, whence he gave the field, which was larger than usual at this period of the year, a preparatory gallop, as a foretaste of the greater pleasures to come when the time arrives for the opening meet, which will be inaugurated at Salthill, near Slough Station. I was very glad to see the Royal Huntsman in improved health, looking, in fact, as fit to go as he has ever been for many a long day. It is pleasant also to hear a good account of the hounds. An outbreak of hydrophobia occurred in the royal kennels at Ascot, during last season, which stopped their hunting for awhile. Much discussion took place as to the course to be pursued under such disastrous circumstances, many being of opinion that the entire pack should be destroyed, in order that the disease might be stamped out. Better counsels prevailed, however, and the noble Master of the Buckhounds, Lord Hardwicke, trusting to the judgment and experience of Frank Goodall, has proved the soundness of his advice, as a finer or more blooming lot of hounds are not to be found. I shall not be far wrong, I think, if I predict a good time for those intending to ride with the Queen's during the ensuing season. The Quorn, though compelled to delay cub-hunting beyond the usual period, owing to the lateness of the harvest, have, nevertheless, been able to kill a youngster or two, giving this fleet pack a taste of blood, as an encouragement to the newly-entered hounds to strive to pull down a gallant old fox when the pace is severe and the country stiff. The greatly-respected master, Mr. Coupland, his numerous friends will regret to hear, is still an invalid. The Cottesmore are rattling the cubs about in the Woodlands; that first-class huntsman, Neale, doing his best to bustle the foxes out of the big covers, so that when the master (Lord Carington) commences the season he may find plenty of the "crafty varmint" in the thick gorse covers, from which many a good run may be safely anticipated. Sir Bache Cunard, having amicably and satisfactorily arranged his differences with the Quorn, is busy at work driving the cubs from Allexton Wood—so that they may afford sure finds to his many supporters in that district. Squire Froude Bellew has already had a good run with his pack—the Dulverton Foxhounds—which hunt that lovely portion of North Devon seen by the tourist when visiting the range of hills known as Hawkridge and the country around Withypool. The well-known pack, the Tedworth, has been hard at work, finding an abundance of cubs. Sir Bellingham Graham—a name as suggestive of bygone days as Melton—has now accepted the office of master of this celebrated pack of foxhounds, made historical from the fact of the Tedworth country having been so long hunted by Assheton Smith. The Marquis of Worcester is busily engaged in the Woodlands scattering the numerous litters, having already killed several, and entered his young hounds early. There is every probability that those who ride over the Duke of Beaufort's grand country will, weather permitting, see good sport, a not unusual state of things in that sporting district. At Brighton Mr. Dewe has commenced hunting regularly three days a week with his fleet pack of harriers over the Downs, and those delighting in a gallop across the open are certain to meet with good sport when visiting the queen of watering-places. The Southdown Foxhounds were out at an early period, and played havoc with the cubs, which abound throughout that country. These hounds are in fine condition and right fit to go, as might be expected from the pains taken with them by Champion, who has carried the horn for upwards of twenty years. The popular master, Mr. Streatfield, is sure to make sport for his numerous followers, as he never goes home whilst there is the smallest chance of showing a run, be the weather what it may, or however late the hour of the day. Several times during last season I can call to mind the hounds having to be whipped off long after darkness had closed "over the Downs so free." The Brookside, by many considered the finest pack of true harriers in the country, will be found as fit as fiddles,

L

and will go the pace up and down the steep hills in the vicinity of Lewes and the surrounding country in their accustomed fine form.

It will be seen by the foregoing account of some of the most celebrated packs that the prospects of sport are decidedly good, always supposing the weather to prove favourable during the ensuing winter. Last year hunting was sadly curtailed by the protracted frost and snow. The country is likely to ride very heavy unless we have some drying winds at the close of this month. The excessive rains have so thoroughly saturated the land that I found, when riding across Exmoor with the Devon and Somerset Staghounds a short while since, it was one vast bog throughout the whole wide district of wild heather-clothed moorland. These hounds, by-the-way, have had grand sport, killing many very heavy stags, after tremendously long runs across the beautiful districts of Devon and Somerset, where the wild red-deer are still to be found in their natural state. The period for hunting the stag has just drawn to a close, and hind-hunting now commences, with every prospect of good sport, as hinds are abundant and in good condition. A visit to this delightful corner of the island will well repay the trouble, especially if the visitor be a thorough sportsman, for an opportunity will be afforded him of whiling away the time until fox-hunting regularly commences, and seeing some grand gallops over the Quantock Hills and the far-stretching, if somewhat treacherous, Exmoor. Now is the time for the followers of the chase to fix upon winter quarters, for the celebrated centres for hunting are rapidly filling up. Melton, the metropolis of sport, will, as usual, be crowded with eager sportsmen and fine studs; nearly every hunting-box is already secured, and those intending to locate themselves in this best of all places for enjoying hunting should lose no time in making their arrangements.

Fortunately, there is no occasion for those with large studs to seek for means of killing time; as they can always enjoy a good gallop every day in the week, either with the Duke of Rutland's pack in the Belvoir country or the Cottesmore, who are kennelled at Barleythorpe, in the centre of one of the best, if not the very best, hunting countries, boasting of some of the finest gorse covers in the world, the celebrated Ranksborough Gorse for one. The most able performers in "the pigskin" will find that it will take them all their time to live with hounds should they run in the direction of Teigh, a line of country not to be excelled, and offering an opportunity of testing the powers of the water-jumpers of the stud when the Whissendine comes in the way, for it is a wide stream, with rotten banks, which require to be negotiated with care. As "Nimrod" pointed out many years since, it is often, and will be found this year certainly, a bumper stream; and "smooth glides the water where the brook is deep," as many an ardent sportsman has found to be the case when trying his hand at jumping it on a shifty nag or a horse that is a little blown or somewhat tired, after half-an-hour's racing across the big pastures, when the fox is making for the well-known cover, Woolwell Head. Above all things, I say to those intending to ride in the shires, see to the condition of your horses; for if they are not right well up to the mark you will not only be unable to live with hounds, but you will be bound to come to grief sooner or later, when sailing, or attempting to sail rather, across the big fields, tall fences, and wide brooks in the shires, on horses that are not fit to go the pace. The well-known adage tells us, "It is the pace that kills," and they do, indeed, go the pace, who ride with these hounds, *vide* such men as the noble master, Lord Carington, Lord Grey de Wilton, Colonel Molineux, Mr. Chandos Pole, Captain Hartopp, Captain Smith, Mr. Lubbock, Sir John Lister Kaye, Lord Wolverton, and Captain Candy, not by any means omitting the ladies, who are found conspicuously to the fore, distinguishing themselves when the hounds round a cracker, to wit, Mrs. Sloane Stanley, Lady Florence Dixie, Mrs. Chaplin, and a host of other well-known personages whom I might name did space permit. The Quorn is always accessible from Melton by those who like a flight across the grass from Holwell Mouth, Gartree Hill, Ashby Pastures, or other of their celebrated "Fixtures," especially when Tom Firr gets well away from the crowd, and lays his hounds on to a stout fox. Sir Bache Cunard, who now hunts the country lately occupied by Mr. Tailby, is also within reach of the residents of Melton, though the distances to cover are somewhat long, but not sufficiently so to prevent good men and true from enjoying the excellent sport that is almost invariably shown in that limited district. Under existing circumstances, therefore, I shall not be far wrong, I think, in predicting a good time for Melton. True it is that the political horizon is somewhat disturbed, and that an amount of gloom is hanging over the agricultural interest; but with a greater allowance of sunshine and more favourable weather than we have experienced during the last two or three years, the British farmer will be all right again. Better times are sure to come round. There is one fact connected with the distress in the agricultural interest that offers a certain amount of consolation to the friends of the farmer—albeit there may be somewhat of selfishness in the thought—that if they give up growing wheat and take to breeding and feeding cattle instead, we, by their kindness, shall find a far larger extent of grass to career across when in pursuit of stag, fox, or hare. That is a consummation to be devoutly wished by the hard rider, who, after a splitting burst of fifty-five minutes without a check, finds, after jumping a tall stake and binder, that he has good sound grass to gallop his tired steed over when going for the finish, instead of the ridge and furrow of a piece of steam-ploughed heavy clay land, enough to break the heart of the best hunter that ever followed the hounds when coming as the finale to a fine run.

So much for Melton and its facilities for sport; but next comes Rugby, one of the most suitable spots in England for those intending to go in for hunting well and conveniently. Situated within two hours' journey from London, by one of the best of railways, the North-Western, the visitor to this inland town has the opportunity of riding with the following crack hounds: the Pytchley, the Atherstone, the North Warwickshire, and also Mr. Tailby's late pack, now the property of Sir Bache Cunard, whose meets are handy to Rugby. Every accommodation is to be obtained in this academical town. Excellent stabling is to be obtained, and when the Pytchley meet at the well-known cover, "Crick" by name, or the North Warwickshire go a cracker from Hillmarton, then the man who follows my advice will admit that he owes me gratitude for the information.

But after indulging so long in generalities, I cannot refrain from entering into particulars of a special good time that I have recently fallen in with. Circumstances having drawn me to the pleasantly-situated town of Tunbridge Wells, whither I had wandered in search of the bucolic—though the picturesque is not wanting in that delightful locality—I made one of the many who attended the show of the Tunbridge Wells Agricultural Association. Under the pleasant tutelage of Mr. J. F. Bates, the occupier of the land upon which the show took place, and with the kindly assistance of Mr. Durrant, the efficient and popular secretary of the Farmers' Club, etc., I was able to inspect the leading articles of the show; and noting the marvellous pens of Southdowns, majestic bulls, stately cows, and prolific pigs, which were exhibited, I formed a rapid conclusion to the effect that it is not all over as yet with the British farmer. Others may have quantity, but he has the quality, as shown by the successful exhibition of agricultural produce. I witnessed the competition for the prize to be given to the best hunter, and watched the Earl of Lewes, Lord George, and Lord Henry Nevill competing, with several others, for the silver cup; and I wondered how Mr. Fitch Kemp and the other judges ever arrived at a conclusion as to which was the best. Roaming amongst the pens of sheep and cattle, I fell in with Lord Abergavenny, and was invited to attend the meet of the West Kent Hounds on the following morning, in order to go cub-hunting in the lovely woods adjacent to Eridge Castle. It is unnecessary to say that I was at the castle in good time.

CHAPTER XXI.

THE HUNTING SEASON.

WHEN this morning dawned great was the stir in the kennels and stables of the three hundred and forty-two packs of stag and fox hounds, harriers and beagles, that hunt over the wide expanse of the United Kingdom; for it is on the first day of November that the hunting season commences in earnest. Notwithstanding the wave of depression that is passing over the agriculturists of the country, it is satisfactory to note that there is no reduction in the number of packs of hounds. Changes there have been, but the total remains precisely the same as that given in our columns three years since. The national sport, fortunately, is too deep-rooted to be affected by what, it may be hoped, is only a temporary run of ill-fortune, due in a measure to the wretched seasons of the past three years, but more to the world-wide competition of foreign countries. If landlord and tenant will pull together, doubtless matters will be adjusted, and we shall see the British farmer "up in the stirrups" once again.

Prospects of sport were never more promising, and from all quarters I hear that foxes are plentiful. During the last two months the huntsmen and whips have been rattling the big coverts, scattering the cubs, and blooding the young hounds. At "the metropolis of hunting," as "Nimrod" so aptly denominated Melton Mowbray, a very good time is expected. Nearly every house and most of the stabling is already engaged, both in the town and its vicinity; while many of the *habitués* of this sporting locality will be found at their favourite resort during the season. Those veteran sportsmen, the Earl of Wilton and Mr. Little Gilmour, who for so many years have made Melton their residence during the hunting season, will be at their accustomed posts in due time.

The Duke of Portland has a large stud, and intends going across the beautiful grass-lands of Leicestershire in proper form, having taken up his abode at the Harboro', with the view of enjoying the pleasant pastime of hunting the fox under the most favourable circumstances, the arrangements of that well-accustomed hotel leaving little to be desired by the most fastidious. Here also will be found Mr. Gilmour, the Marquis of Queensberry, Messrs. Horace and Lewis Flower, Captain Hill Trevor, and others, whilst in the vicinity the Hon. Hugh and Lady Grace Lowther, with Sir Beaumont and Lady Florence Dixie, will be found as usual, together with a host of hard riders who annually visit Melton for the purpose of enjoying the sport and joining in the pleasant society which has ever been the charm of this fashionable resort since the days when "Nimrod" so graphically described it in the "Quarterly Review."

At Oakham, the capital of Redlandshire—or, as we call it now, Rutlandshire—houses and stabling are in request, its close proximity to Barleythorpe, where the kennels and stables of the Cottesmore are situated, making it a convenient locality for such as hunt with these hounds. It is here that Custance, after a long and successful career on the turf, has located himself, carrying on the business of one of the first-class hotels. But it is at Melton that fox-hunting is to be enjoyed to the fullest extent. Every day in the week one or other of the splendid packs that hunt the cream of the shires meets within reach. To-day the Duke of Rutland's beautiful pack begins at Harlaxton Hall, and it will be a strange thing if Frank Gillard, the energetic huntsman of the Belvoir, does not show the large "field" that is sure to be present on the first day of the season a rattling good run over

> The russet lawns and fallows gray
> Where the nibbling flocks do stray.

The master of the Belvoir can boast of possessing sixty-two couples of the best hounds in the world, to be excelled by none for shape, uniformity, colour, and condition. The fixture of the Quorn to-day is the historical "Kirby Gate," where "Tom Firr" will bring his racing hounds; and, should they run a clinker across the big pastures of this fine "country," the "field" allowing them to get well away from the cover before they sit down to ride, it will be only good men that will be able to live with them. The ground, after the heavy rain which has fallen, is bound to ride badly, the brooks will be "bumpers," the fences somewhat blind, and the pace severe, should the scent lie well. The popular master of the Quorn, Mr. John Coupland, a thorough sportsman and a rare good man across country, has fifty-five couples of splendid hounds, with which he will hunt five days a week.

The Cottesmore, of which Mr. W. Baird is now the master—replacing that first-rate and excellent sportsman Lord Carington, whose retirement was so deeply regretted—meet at the well-known Greetham Inn; and Neal, the persevering, hard-riding, and good-tempered huntsman of this brilliant pack, will show the riders the way to get over the country, should he find a fox that points his head straight and faces the open. He will be a good man who overrides these hounds if they get well away and settle down to their fox, as my experience has proved. There is little doubt that the Hon. Hugh Lowther will be "all there" on this the opening day; and should any enterprising stranger elect to follow him over the grass, he will be a very fortunate man if he does not come to grief, for it must be a very stiff flight of posts and rails, a very tall bullfinch, or a wide, deep, and swift-running stream that will stop that resolute rider when hounds go the pace over one of the finest countries in the world. Not to have met these hounds at Ranksborough Gorse, not to have tried a gallop across the big grass-fields, and a shy at the Whissendine, is to proclaim yourself out of the running altogether, if you would be considered a thorough sportsman. The fixtures of Sir Bache Cunard's hounds are generally rather wide of Melton, but yet within reach. A galloping hack, or a pair of posters from The George, will always accomplish the distance easily enough. This morning the meet is at Bosworth, and a large contingent of hard-riding men from Rugby and Market Harborough will doubtless be present. The unfortunate dispute which arose when Mr. Tailby gave up his hounds, as to possession of this country, has been amicably arranged, and the riders with this pack are to be congratulated upon having got a master who does the thing in such good form.

From Rugby I hear the prospects of the season are brilliant. The Pytchley, of which Mr. H. H. Langham is master, has fifty-six couples of first-class hounds with which to hunt the country four days a week. The pack is said to be in fine form, and "Will Goodall" may be trusted to show plenty of sport as usual, while those who want to see "how the thing is done" should attend one of the several crack meets of this noted pack which this week offers. To-day the fixture is "Sywell Wood," and such as visit this fine fox-hunting country must be prepared to harden their hearts, hustle their horses, and go full tilt at the big fences, if they intend to live to hounds.

The Atherstone meet to-day at Bosworth, and Mr. W. E. Oakeley has fifty-four couples of noble hounds with which he proposes to show sport four days a week. It will not be the fault of his persevering huntsman, George Castleman, if he does not show the "field" a rattling run over this sporting country, where the fences are sufficiently big to satisfy the most ardent sportsman, and test his powers of going to hounds.

The meet of the North Warwickshire for this day is Stoneleigh Abbey, that well-known sportsman, Mr. Richard Lant, being the master, and W. Wheatley, a thorough good man, the huntsman, who has fifty couples of good useful hounds with which to hunt the country. The visitors at Rugby have therefore three first-class packs within reach, and, unless there is a strong departure from the usual custom, right good sport may safely be depended upon. The principal hotel, the Royal George, has, as usual, many visitors, amongst whom occur the well-known names of Count Metternich, Mr. Shiel, Mr. W. N. Heysham, Captain Scott, Mr. Hopcroft, etc., all attracted by the comforts and conveniences of this well-known establishment. In the town are located Mr. Yarborough, Mr. Seabright, Mr. Dalgleish, Mr. Swaley, Mr. Shoolbred, and sundry other hard-riding men, who enjoy the clinking runs of this convenient centre of the Midland Counties. Foxes are abundant in this district, hares somewhat scarce, and likely soon to be scarcer.

The Duke of Beaufort's noble pack is in full force, numbering seventy-five couples of magnificent hounds, with which the Marquis of Worcester will hunt the country five days a week. When last I visited Badminton kennels I recognised what a perfect hound should be, and the description of the well-known Mr. Meynell of former days, designated by "Nimrod" as the "Father of the modern chase," was fully realised when I observed the short backs, open bosoms, straight legs, and compact feet which he determined to be the proper form of the foxhound. The country hunted by the Duke of Beaufort requires powerful hounds, the fences being big, and the country in parts hilly, with stone walls here and there, which require clever nags to surmount. If Janus, which was knocked down to Lord Arthur Somerset the other day at the sale at Cricklewood of the Andover and Wey Hill Company's hunters, should be destined for the Duke of Beaufort, he may safely be depended upon to carry any reasonable weight over any country—for a more perfect specimen of a weight-carrier I have never seen. To stay at Bath, and hunt with the Badminton Hounds, I consider to be as near perfect happiness as is permitted to mortals—those of sporting tendencies be it understood.

Great excitement has been created amongst residents in the vicinity of High Wycombe by the fact of Lord Carington having taken over for a time the superb pack of bloodhounds the property of Lord Wolverton. Truly grand are the performances of this, the only pack of the breed in the country, and whoever sees them going in pursuit of a sturdy stag over that light-riding country will have a rare treat. Then he will hear the deep tones of these most musical hounds, as he watches them carefully hunting the deer, not hastily, but steadily pursuing their object with a diligent persistence for probably two hours or even more, and surely running into their quarry at last. In the hands of such a sportsman as the present master, marvellous days may safely be predicted.

The South Oxfordshire Hounds, of which the veteran sportsman and greatly and deservedly respected master is the Earl of Macclesfield, meet at Shirburn Castle this day. Though "the inaudible and noiseless foot of time" has set its imprint somewhat deeply upon him, yet the noble master of this celebrated pack will carry the horn with his accustomed skill, and show the usual good results of long practical experience in hunting the fox. The Duke of Grafton's hounds, which number fifty couples, of what I believe to be the fastest hounds in England, are kennelled at Wakefield Lawn, Stony Stratford, and are under the care of Frank Beers, a name well known in hunting circles for many a long year past. This is a historic pack, and must be seen to be fully appreciated, but should the sportsman be disposed to try a day with them, and should he perchance drop in with a burst of twenty-five minutes, as I did, he will find it will take all his science to keep in the front rank, however well he may be mounted. The Bicester and Warden Hill Hounds, of which Viscount Valentia is master, and R. Stovin the huntsman, meet on Tuesday at Charlton Townend, and will give those who visit Bicester, Buckingham, Brackley, or Banbury, an opportunity of riding over some of the magnificent country hunted by this well-known pack. The Blankney, Mr. Henry Chaplin, the well-known sportsman, being the master, and Henry Dawkins the huntsman, consists of· fifty couples of high-bred hounds, and those who visit the sporting county of Lincoln may depend upon witnessing some fine runs. The fixture to-day is Southrey, and though the ground must necessarily be deep after the heavy rainfall, it will not stop the Lincolnshire lads from going the pace. The fixture for Lord Fitzhardinge's noted pack for this morning is Alveston Ship, and those who visit Berkeley, Dursley, or Thornbury, in Gloucestershire, will see as fine a pack of hounds as can be found, numbering sixty-five and a half couples in all, under the care of Ben Barlow, which show rare sport to the good men and true who follow them over the hills and dales, stone walls, and running brooks of that pleasant county. Those who have sojourned at the celebrated inn known as The Haycock, at "Wansford, in England," will do well to revisit that pleasant place of entertainment, and ride with the Fitzwilliam, as an opportunity is offered this week of seeing this celebrated pack perform over some of the best parts of their country.

To-day the meet is at the kennels, at Milton, near Peterborough, when a host of well-known riders will put in an appearance. On the retirement of the Marquis of Huntly, the Hon. T. Wentworth Fitzwilliam accepted the responsibility of the mastership of this crack pack, and as he has George Carter, the apt pupil of the celebrated Tom Sebright, for his huntsman, a grand lot of hounds, and a truly fine hunting country, there is little doubt that he will fully maintain the prestige of the Fitzwilliam.

Journeying towards the south coast, the follower of the Southdown Foxhounds will find his friends and fellow-sportsmen commencing the season to-day with a public breakfast at the kennels at Ringmer. George Champion, having under his charge fifty couples of beautiful hounds, is one of the most persevering huntsmen I have ever ridden with, and no one can beat him at puzzling out the line of a fox over the downs when the weather is bad and the scent indifferent. The Brighton Harriers will also well repay a visit. Their season has already commenced, and they have had some capital spins over the downs. A visit a few weeks back to the new kennels at Patcham satisfied me that no better hounds could be found for this country. Every one is a foxhound drafted from the best kennels in England, and entered to hare. Mr. Dewe, the master, may well be proud of his even, handsome, clever pack. The Brookside Harriers are in good form, and any judge of hare-hunting will be delighted with Mr. Steyning Beard's lot of true-bred harriers.

The first meet of the West Kent Foxhounds takes place this day at Birling Manor, the ancient family seat of the Nevills. The master, the Hon. Ralph Pelham Nevill, will entertain all comers at breakfast, afterwards an opportunity will be afforded of seeing that clever and persevering huntsman, George Bollen, perform with his handsome lot of hounds. Earl Ferrers' brilliant pack meet for the first time to-day at Belton, when his lordship, who hunts the hounds himself over the country in the vicinity of Ashby-de-la-Zouch, will not fail to pull down a stout fox if he has a chance. This, though a small pack—twenty-five couples in all—hunting a limited tract of country, is, in the opinion of some—the best judges of fox-hunting —one of the best in England.

The York and Ainsty, of which Captain Slingsby is now the master, consists of fifty couples of good-looking hounds, hunting the country around York four days a-week, commencing to-day at Strensall. Travelling farther northward, the celebrated and popular sportsman, Colonel I. Anstruther Thomson, the Master of the Fife Hounds, will be at Pitcarlie this morning. In the lovely county of Devonshire those who enjoy riding over hill, dale, and moorland will find the Dartmoor Hounds at Ivy Bridge, the South Devon at Ainbrook, and the noted Dulverton pack at Swineham Hill this day; and I venture to say that those who ride with Mr. Froude Bellew, the master of the latter, will be charmed with the loveliness of the scenery and delighted with the air on the heather-clad hills. In the sporting eastern county four packs will be found of first-rate hounds. The Essex, of which Sir H. Selwin-Ibbetson is master, meeting to-day at Matching Green; the East Essex, Lieutenant-Colonel Jelf Sharp master, at Abbot's Hall; the Essex Union, Mr. Carnegie master, at Rochford Lawn; and the Essex and Suffolk, Mr. T. W. Nunn master, at Elmstead Market on Tuesday. In Surrey four packs will commence business—the Old Surrey, which hunts the country around Croydon and Godstone; the Surrey Union, around Epsom and Dorking; the excellent pack of staghounds which are now kennelled at Nutfield; and Mr. Farnell Watson's staghounds, which hunt the country around Dorking and Horsham. The fixtures of these packs are not advertised, the fear being, if they were, that there would be too large an attendance.

In Wales the superb pack of Sir Watkin Williams Wynn, which are housed at Wynstay, consisting of sixty couples of high-bred hounds, will commence the season on Tuesday at Rednall. A visit to this fine pack will be a rare treat to any lover of the noble sport who has not as yet seen them. In Cheshire, Captain Park Yates will appear with his pack, which hunts in the vicinity of Northwich, Chester, and Tarporley, and Mr. H. Reginald Corbet, of the South Cheshire—a name celebrated in the annals of fox-hunting—will carry the horn, hunting his hounds in right good form. Did space permit I could write of many more excellent packs of hounds, but as I must reserve a place for the crack packs of staghounds, I most unwillingly curtail my experiences, gained by fifty-two years' devotion to the manly and noble sport.

In the Vale of Aylesbury, Sir Nathaniel de Rothschild will give hard-goers a chance of riding over his brilliant pack of hounds, if they can. When an hour has passed across the Vale, I venture to predict that Fred Cox, who has hunted these hounds for three or four and twenty years, will find "the field" reduced to a select few, looking at the state of the country after the heavy rains and floods. In Hertfordshire, Mr. Richard Rawle will, as usual, show some first-rate sport, chasing the deer over the open country around Berkhampstead, Tring, and St. Albans. Across the Roodings of Essex, the Hon. H. W. Petre will enable those who like to go the pace, and are not afraid of the wide ditches that are the feature of the country, to try how long they can live to hounds when they have a stout deer before them.

Last, but not least, in the category of first-class hounds, are those of Her Majesty. These Royal Buckhounds, of which the Earl of Cork and Orrery is now the master, will meet on Tuesday, according to time-honoured custom, at Salt Hill. After some weeks of forest-hunting, Frank Goodall, whose marvellous care and attention to the fine hounds under his care must be seen to be duly appreciated, will show as handsome and useful a lot as can be found in Her Majesty's dominions.

CHAPTER XXII.

STAGE-COACHES OF THE PERIOD.

NOT one of the popular amusements of the season has suffered more from the unsettled state of the elements than has the rejuvenescent custom of coaching; and this is the more unfortunate since preparations for a happy return to the olden ways had been made on a greatly-extended scale, no fewer than sixteen well-appointed four-horse stage-coaches having been put on the road for the accommodation and pleasure of the public. First and foremost of these stage-coaches is the Defiance, which travels between the two universities, leaving The Mitre at Oxford every Monday, Wednesday, and Friday, going *viâ* High Wycombe, London, and Royston, and returning from the Bull Hotel, Cambridge, every Tuesday, Thursday, and Saturday, the distance—112 miles—being accomplished in twelve hours, including stoppages. The proprietor of the Defiance is Mr. Carleton Blyth, who has spared no expense to make his large venture a success. At starting he informed me that he had provided as many as 120 horses, of an exceedingly good stamp; whilst his coaches, of Holland's build, are models, in shape, style, colour, and finish, of what stage-coaches should be, and are equal, if not superior, to any that were seen in the palmiest days of the road. When the skies have permitted pleasure-folks to travel, the Defiance has carried good loads; and now that there is an appearance of a continuance of settled weather, an opportunity will be afforded of fetching up some of the leeway. That the venture is a costly one will readily be understood by any conversant with coaching matters. The first cost of this large stud, together with the coaches, harness, and stable requisites, involves a large outlay, and I shall not be very far from the mark if I fix the amount of capital invested in the Defiance at about 10,000*l*. Throughout the entire length of the long journey, this first-class stage-coach of the period, the Defiance, is worked in a style that deserves success, though in the teeth of this disastrous season it cannot command it. The spirited proprietor, however, is not easily daunted, and it is to be hoped that his motto will be, "Better luck next time."

A very cheery hour can be passed at the celebrated old coaching rendezvous, the White Horse Cellar, Piccadilly; say from 10.30 to 11.30 A.M., whilst watching the coming and going of the different well-appointed stages. Shortly before the advertised hour the clear notes of the well-blown horns announce the coming in different directions of the thoroughly business-like drag which works between Hatchett's and Windsor, and the excellently-horsed Box Hill coach, both being timed to leave the Cellar each day at 10.30. At 10.45 the "Tally Ho!" starts for Virginia Water, and performs the journey through a beautiful line of country in excellent style, being well horsed throughout and cleverly worked by the two enterprising proprietors. The Sevenoaks coach, which was timed for a short season to leave Piccadilly at 10.45, was withdrawn at an early period in consequence of the departure for the Continent of Baron Schröder, who worked it in conjunction with Lord Helmsley. The public, therefore, lose the pleasure of journeying along this pleasant route, of witnessing the first-rate form in which the business was carried on, and of admiring the crack lot of nags which were employed, as well as the workmanlike way in which they were handled. At 11 o'clock an opportunity of observing the Guildford coach is afforded, and as it draws up in front of Hatchett's it is evident at a glance that no pains have been spared to turn it out in real coaching form. The horses are well chosen and matched, and when Mr. Walter Shoolbred moves off, you see that an artist is on the bench. If you accompany him on this delightful journey you will find, throughout the whole distance, everything done in proper form, and will mark the marvellous punctuality on arriving at the end of the different stages. This denotes a coachman; for, without regularity of pace, the necessity of making up time occurs, and that, with a heavy load, causes great and unnecessary distress to a team.

At 11.15 the Perseverance, owned, and worked in admirable style, by Mr. Sheather, leaves for Dorking, and frequently carries good loads to its pleasant place of destination. I must not, however, omit to say that, prior to the starting of the Perseverance, the departure of the Old Times is a sight not to be missed. The coach in question runs to St. Alban's, returning each day (Sundays, of course, excepted, as is the rule with all the coaches leaving the Cellar), from the George Hotel, at 4 P.M. This is a real stage-coach, running throughout the winter, the severity of which did not appal Major Dixon, nor discourage Selby, who braved the pitiless pelting of many storms. At 12 o'clock on every Tuesday, Thursday, and Saturday, what may be well called, to use the advertised term, "a fast four-horse coach" leaves the Cellar for Brighton, arriving at the Old Ship Hotel at 6 o'clock, doing the journey throughout at a rattling pace of eleven and a-half miles an hour. Arriving at this well-known hostelry, the visitor may take · the word of one who has frequented it, any time these fifty years, that he will fare right well. Every day during the season a capital coach is worked between the Ranelagh and Hurlingham Clubs, doing the distance in 35 minutes; but the disastrous season so affected the attendance at these fashionable resorts that the balance will be found, I fear, on the wrong side of the ledger. Day after day did the heavy downpour spoil the pleasure and limit the company at the Ranelagh; and notwithstanding the great exertions of Mr. Reginald Herbert to provide high-class amusements, it must have been anything but a profitable business this year.

After the departure of the Ranelagh coach there has daily been a lull until 4 o'clock, at which hour Mr. Robinson's admirably turned-out coach leaves for Thames Ditton, going by way of Kew, Teddington, and Hampton Court, and reaching the Swan Hotel at 7.50. This is a lovely ride, terminating in time for the passenger, if he so desires, to return to London by train, after enjoying a capital dinner at the pleasant waterside hotel so well known to boating-men. No better turn-out leaves The Cellar than that of Mr. Robinson. His first-class coach is of Holland's make, and is admirably horsed, notably in the first stage. Four finer coach-horses than those working from Hatchett's cannot be found, and the coachmanship is in accordance with the rest of the arrangements. At 4.30 the Beckenham coach starts, usually with a good load, and travels smartly, arriving at Beckenham at 6 o'clock, and finishing its journey, a most delightful one, at West Wickham. This also is a well-horsed and capitally-worked coach, of which Selby is the professional whip; and the traveller will find himself amply repaid for the time expended in seeing how the thing is done—always supposing him to be an admirer of artists on the bench. In addition to the foregoing list, a coach has been running from the Horseshoe Hotel, in Tottenham Court Road, every morning at 11 o'clock, passing through Roehampton, Barnes, Wimbledon, and Kingston, arriving at Hampton at 1.15 P.M., returning from thence at 4.15; also one from the St. James's Hall, Piccadilly, every afternoon (Sundays included) at 5.15, for the Ship and Trafalgar Hotels, at Greenwich, returning at 10.15. In the country, the well-known fast and splendidly-appointed Hirondelle works from the George Inn, Enfield, to The Sun at Hitchin, travelling by way of Hatfield Park and Welwyn, and doing the journey at a slapping pace, admirably worked by that first-class whip, Colonel Plantagenet Somerset. Between Oxford and Cheltenham the Blenheim is worked by Mr. Augustus Craven, assisted by the veteran Harry Ward, who, on the termination of his engagement on the Sevenoaks coach, transferred his services to the proprietor of the Blenheim. This coach leaves the Mitre Hotel, Oxford, every Monday, Wednesday, and Friday, at 2.30; travels through Ensham, Witney, North Leach, and Andoversford; and reaches Cheltenham at 7 o'clock, doing the distance— $40\frac{1}{4}$ miles—in four and a-half hours. This will be found a very pleasant journey, and anyone wishing for an opportunity of seeing the route between London and Cheltenham, can, by travelling from Hatchett's by Mr. Carleton Blyth's coach, resting a night at Oxford, and journeying on the following day to Cheltenham, reach that fashionable watering-place without fatigue or trouble. The trip commends itself to ladies who indulge in the pleasant pastime of travelling by coach through districts and towns not visible when journeying by rail.

Like everyone else, my opportunities of travelling on the different coaches have been limited by the tempestuous times that have so unfortunately spoiled all the pleasures of the spring and summer; but notwithstanding the opposition of the elements, I have succeeded in making some agreeable journeys. My first venture was on the Windsor coach, having been invited by Mr. Bailey to accompany him on that pleasant route. Fortunately, on this occasion, the weather was propitious for once in a way, and we started with a full load at 10.30 sharp; passed through Kew, where the first change was made; then away by Richmond, Twickenham, Teddington, and Bushey Park; pulling up at The King's Arms precisely at noon. Off again, we soon rattled into Hampton, changed horses at The Red Lion, and then, after a sharp spin, pulled up at The Angel at Staines, where the third change took place. Thence we trotted away at a lively pace, and reached the well-known White Hart Hotel precisely to time. One of the noticeable pleasures of travelling by coach is the congenial company you fall in with during the journey. On this occasion several ladies accompanied us, and added greatly to the delight of the ride by their pleasant manners.

After lunching at The White Hart, the return journey commenced at 3.40, Hatchett's being reached at 6.50. This is one of the pleasantest rides of the many offered to the public; and the opportunity is still available, now that there is some appearance of fine weather, of visiting Windsor in a comfortable way. The coach is well horsed, and Mr. Bailey is a thorough coachman, by whose side it is a pleasure to sit.

On another occasion, when the day was bright and clear, I took my place on the "Tally Ho!" and journeyed to The Wheat Sheaf at Virginia Water. This being the first trip, the horses were very fresh, requiring careful handling on the part of the two proprietors, who worked the up and down journeys between them. Leaving the Cellar at 10.45, travelling at a rapid rate, The Red Lion at Barnes is reached, where the first change is made; then away through Richmond, Bushey Park, changing a second time at The King's Arms, Hampton Court; on by Walton, past Oaklands Park and Weybridge; then, changing again at The Swan at Chertsey, we arrive at Virginia Water at 1.45, to find a capital luncheon awaiting us at The Wheat Sheaf. Again I was fortunate in falling in with agreeable fellow-travellers, several ladies being of the party.

After resting in the picturesque locality for two hours, the return journey commenced, and we trotted along merrily, arriving at The Cellar at 6.45, after a most thoroughly enjoyable ride. Having had so good a time on these two journeys, I readily accepted an invitation to accompany Baron Schröder to Sevenoaks.

On arriving in Piccadilly, I found Harry Ward in charge of the well-appointed coach and four fresh well-bred horses, and we were speedily trotting away, travelling along the Vauxhall Bridge Road, where the traffic is sadly disarranged by the double lines of tramway; thence to The Greyhound at Dulwich, where we changed horses; then up the steep hill that brings you to the Crystal Palace; through Bromley, changing the team there, going on to The Polhill Arms, where a very handsome lot of nags were put to, and pulled us in good style up the steep hill which you have to mount in order to reach Sevenoaks.

The different teams were cleverly and carefully handled by Baron Schröder, who had got his lot of valuable young horses in capital form. This is a lovely journey throughout. Again I was fortunate in meeting with pleasant fellow-travellers, one of whom, bearing the honoured name of a great modern statesman, occupied the box-seat on this occasion.

A friend on whose judgment I could thoroughly rely having informed me that I should be gladly welcomed if I introduced myself to Mr. Robinson, who has put on the coach which plies between Hatchett's and the Swan Hotel at Thames Ditton, and should find it a first-rate turn-out and delightful ride, I duly presented myself at the starting-point at 6 o'clock, and was tooled in excellent style and at a slapping pace to The Cumberland Arms, opposite Kew Gardens, where we changed horses, having thence a team of capital working nags, if not as handsome and valuable as the first team to which I have already alluded. Again the evening was fine, and the ride particularly pleasant. A large party filled the coach, and on arrival at The Swan were hospitably entertained by the proprietor of the first-class stage-coach, returning by train to London.

An opportunity being offered of travelling with Mr. Freeman to Brighton, on his well-known coach, I jumped at the chance, always glad of any excuse for visiting that charming city by the sea. Making my way to Hatchett's at 12 o'clock on Saturday, I found a full load, the only vacant place being the box-seat, which had been kindly retained for me, and, jumping up, we were speedily traversing Piccadilly, passing soon through Brixton, and making our first halt at Streatham; then at a rapid rate, the coach being timed to do the journey at the speed of eleven and a-half miles an hour, and, keeping it punctually to the minute, we reached Caterham Junction, where we made our second change; then with little delay we were away again, rising Redhill, and making for Horley; half an hour being allowed for luncheon at The Chequers, the old-fashioned roadside inn, familiar to all surviving roadsters, who were accustomed to travel this route ere railways had for so long a time put a stop to coaching. After partaking of the profusion of good things provided by the careful hostess of The Chequers, we resumed our journey. All through the distance this coach is admirably horsed, and when Mr. Freeman springs his high-mettled horses. up the rising ground, galloping at full speed, the coach travelling as steadily as possible, you feel that you are sitting by the side of an accomplished whip. Most exhilarating is a spurt like this, when you have confidence in the coachman who can take a liberty with his team. Passing by way of Handcross we reach Cuckfield, where we change again, and then, on by Friar's Oak, run into Brighton, where we arrive at The Old Ship as the hand on the clock points to six, the hour fixed.

Brighton is seen at its best, and I am glad to hear there is every prospect of a good season, more houses being let at this early period than have been for several years past. At 12 o'clock on Monday the coach drew up, the ribbons being handled on the return journey by that consummate artist, J. Thorogood, by whose side it is a treat to sit and watch the quiet way in which he handles his horses. Never mind how fresh they may be—and the Brighton coach-horses are fresh, and in fine condition too—they soon subside and settle down to their work; and again we are going the pace, Thorogood following Mr. Freeman's example, springing his willing horses on every bit of rising ground, and keeping time to a minute at every stage. At Croydon Mr. Chandos Pole met us and took the reins for the stage into London, handling the splendid team that works this part of the ground in right good form, proving himself to be as good on the bench as he is in the saddle when sailing across Leicestershire. Colonel Stacey Clitheroe is joint proprietor of the coach with Mr. Freeman, and this pleasant journey is performed throughout in first-rate style, and offers an opportunity for those who like to see four good horses handled in proper form, and taking a lesson in coaching as well as enjoying for a few hours the invigorating air of Brighton. In order to maintain the high speed at which this coach is worked, the stages are short, and the number of horses required to work the road is thirty-six—every one being well suited to its place. Now that the weather is to some extent improved there is yet time to try a trip on any one of the fourteen stage-coaches still running, and I know of no pleasanter way of spending a few days than by travelling in this fashion along the routes which I have named. Of the increasing popularity of coaching an instance is afforded by the notification of an arrangement for the working of a coach by Mr. Geo. Cox, between Hatchett's and The Lion at Farningham, *viâ* Bromley and Chiselhurst, at an early period of the ensuing spring.

CHAPTER XXIII.

BY ROAD TO BRIGHTON.

THERE is no more agreeable way, to my mind, of journeying to the queen of watering-places than by securing the box-seat on one of the admirably-appointed stage-coaches that run between Piccadilly and Brighton. The spirited proprietors of these excellently-horsed, well and carefully driven vehicles, should have a greater amount of support than is accorded to them by the visitors to this fashionable resort. The fearful railway accidents that have recently occurred will deal a heavy blow and great discouragement to the proprietors of the iron horses of the country, unless they improve a system of management that allows such calamities to be possible. For my part, I am convinced that the well-known proverb that "Hurry is the Devil" showed the Arabs to be a highly intelligent people; and impressed with this view, when contemplating a visit to Brighton, I decided, as I was only on pleasure bent, that I would accept Mr. Freeman's invitation to occupy the box-seat, and be conveyed to my destination by four quick-stepping nags, rather than be whirled through the air by an express train. It must be remembered that there was a great amount of truth in the description of the difference between railway accidents and those by coaches, given by old Will Bowers, the noted Oxford coachman, to Sir Henry Peyton, when they were discussing the subject in the early days of travelling by steam. "If," said that admitted authority, "an accident happens to a coach, why there you are; but if an accident occurs to a train, where are you?" Reflecting on the truth of this old and trite observation, and feeling that in my case " Hurry would be the Devil," I decided on travelling safely and leisurely along the road, and witnessing the way in which a first-rate coachman handled the ribbons and tooled the different teams from stage to stage, with the minutest punctuality, which experience taught me would be the case. Choosing Saturday last for my journey, I left home in a heavy downpour that showed no signs of cessation. Fortunately, before I reached The Cellar a rift appeared in the clouds, then the sun emerged from the gloom, bits of blue sky were visible, and for the remainder of the day all went merry as a marriage-bell.

The Brighton coaches are driven alternately by Mr. W. Stewart Freeman, Colonel Clitheroe, Mr. Anson, and Lord Algernon Lennox. In the absence of the proprietors, then Thorogood, the professional coachman, occupies the bench, doing so on this occasion, and performing the journey with his accustomed punctuality, arriving at The Old Ship as the hand of the clock pointed to a quarter-past six—the appointed time—notwithstanding the fact of his losing some twelve or fifteen minutes by the troublesome conduct of one of the second team, whom, however, he subdued and made do its part of the work, keeping his temper thoroughly, though tried by some of the vagaries of the wilful animal. Taking my seat, I found six or seven passengers had like myself determined to chance the weather and travel by road. Starting to the minute, we trotted gaily along Piccadilly, down to Grosvenor Place, the four chestnuts stepping well together; then Grosvenor Gardens being reached, I observed Mr. Robert Percivall, the well-known horse dealer of South Eaton Place, seated on an American waggon, in the shafts of which was a bloodlike chestnut mare, barely fifteen hands high, which I had been told he intended to drive from London to Brighton, doing the distance throughout in the same time as the coach. Sitting by his side was the well-known form of Tim Carter, the two together making up a dead weight of over twenty stone. On the passing of the coach, the little mare, " Multum in Parvo " (the name under which she distinguished herself in her native country — America) started steadily on her long journey, stepping in capital form, and looking, though not specially prepared for the journey, as fit as a fiddle, her performance fully carrying out this promise, as subsequent events proved. On our arrival at Streatham we changed horses for the first time, the little mare keeping behind the coach; but on arriving at Thornton Heath the mare was trotted ahead, and on our arrival at Horley at a quarter to three we found her in the stable, having performed her task thus far with consummate ease.

At this point the up Brighton coach, tooled by that crack coachman, Harry Ward, pulled up to the minute, the two coaches being timed to meet at The

Chequers, where luncheon was prepared on a liberal scale for the passengers, who were not slow to avail themselves of the opportunity of enjoying the many good things prepared for them, recalling the old coaching-days, when the roadside inn was an institution of the country. On the expiration of the twenty minutes, which is the time allowed for refreshment, we were off again, "Multum in Parvo" this time going ahead, giving me the opportunity of seeing the excellent action and steady going which enable her to get over the ground with so much ease. Keeping in sight of us until we turned out of the main-road to change horses at Peas Porridge, then going along at a smart pace, we saw nothing more of her until we reached Brighton, where she had arrived a quarter of an hour before us. From Peas Porridge we went at a rattling pace, Thorogood springing the team over parts of the road, the coach travelling as steady as a die, though the pace was severe. Then Cuckfield was reached, where we changed horses for the fifth time; on this occasion the team being short-legged cobby animals, one a remarkably useful Welsh mare, that looked like going far and fast, without trouble to herself. At length Friars Oak is reached, and we change for the sixth and last time, and start off with a capital team of good-looking well-bred grays.

So far we had escaped any rain, but now we were threatened with a heavy storm, which, however, passed over the downs, and we reached our destination without being drenched to the skin, as seemed at one time very likely to be the case. Pulling up to the instant, as before described, we found the customary group of loungers awaiting the arrival of the Brighton and

London and Brighton and Arundel coaches, both of which start from the well-known hostelry so long and pleasantly conducted by Messrs. Bacon.

Amongst those awaiting our arrival were Mr. Robert Percivall and his companion Tim Carter, who had done the distance without distressing the mare one jot. Being desirous of seeing "Multum in Parvo" after her journey, I accompanied Mr. Percivall to Mannington's stables, where I found her being dressed, after drinking some gruel, and she looked as fit to start on the return journey as she did when I first observed her in Grosvenor Gardens. However, this she was not called upon to do, but remained in her stable until Monday morning, when Carter drove her steadily back, but not until Messrs. Hennah and Kent had photographed the group in their accustomed excellent style, at whose establishment, by-the-way, in the King's Road, I saw a group of short-horn cattle, so beautifully taken as to form a most pleasing picture, and also a lifelike portrait of Isonomy, the admirers of which noble animal should hasten to inspect the resemblance of their favourite.

This clever and enduring animal, which Mr. Percivall exhibited, was, I am told, purchased at a very high price; her powers of endurance and clever style of going being well-known on the other side of the water; and it is likely that a match will be made ere long, that she may further exhibit her powers by doing the same distance in an unprecedentedly short time. This, if her powers are not too severely taxed, will be an interesting trial; and as Mr. Percivall's long experience and success in trotting-matches are very well known, it may safely be left to his judgment not to call upon the willing little mare to do more than she can satisfactorily perform.

For powers of endurance we must trust entirely to blood; half-bred ones will not stay. It must be blood, and good blood too, to exhibit that quality in the right good form that the little mare did; and that appears to be fully recognised nowadays by our American cousins, if I may judge by some of the specimens that have been sent to the old country. They are beginning to see the value of breeding and training horses that can bend their knees and step away, finding those animals who can only "pace" are not suitable for the English market, though they are more appreciated on the Continent. There is no doubt that if attention is paid to this point the trade between the two countries in this class of horses will be continuous and increasing. Persons desirous of exchanging the dull and dirty ways of the gloomy metropolis for sunshine and fresh air should decide upon Brighton; then, if they recognise the fact that "Hurry is the Devil," and going steadily down the road, on the box of one of these well-appointed stages, should find themselves sitting down to an excellent and well-served dinner at The New Ship, meeting with a host of pleasant companions, as I did, they will thank me for the suggestion that they should travel "By Road to Brighton."

CHAPTER XXIV.

AN AUTUMN TOUR THROUGH NORTH DEVON AND SOMERSET.

DURING the entire month of October any lover of English scenery, who has a week or fortnight to spare, may luxuriate amongst the most beautiful landscapes that are to be found in the lovely counties of Devon and Somerset. Grander scenery may be found in many parts of England, but nothing more beautiful than that which is within easy reach and approachable under the most favourable circumstances. Starting by the Great Western or South-Western Railways, Taunton is reached in about four hours and a half. Excellent accommodation is to be found at the Railway Hotel opposite to the exit-gate from the down platform. Here conveyances may be hired, and the route over the Quantox Hills to the Bristol Channel arranged; or, if travelling by rail is preferred, the line runs direct from Taunton to Minehead, passing by way of Combe Florey, Stogumber, Watchet, and Dunster. Should, however, an intending visitor, trusting to his own powers of locomotion, prefer to walk over this lovely country, the distance to be traversed before reaching the shores of the Bristol Channel will not exceed twenty miles. Either when riding or walking, a vast panorama of smiling country is visible whichever way the eye turns; on one side of this heather-clad range of grand hills is seen the surrounding rich Vale of Taunton; on the other side the view extends over Bridgewater Bay to Burnham and Weston-super-Mare; whilst following the line of hills which trend down to the Channel, a view of the Welsh coast is obtained. The prominent feature of these parts are the Combes, which may be described as verdant valleys, the hillsides of which are densely clothed with the redundant foliage of beautiful beeches and other luxuriant trees, which flourish so greatly in these parts. It is amidst these tranquil woodlands that the wild red-deer are found in their natural state, and these graceful animals roam at will over hill, dale, and moorland, affording grand sport to the lover of the chase, who follows them over the Quantox Hills, or the wild trackless waste of Exmoor, frequently pursuing the stag until he seeks refuge in the waters of the Channel.

> When the headland is reached from the tall cliff he bounds,
> And in the wild ocean escapes from the hounds;
> Then, resigned to his fate, o'er the waters he's borne,
> And dies on the wild wave that breaks on Glenthorn,

one of the loveliest spots on the coast of North Devon.

Arriving at Quantox Head, the visitor should seek for St. Andries House, the residence of Sir Alexander Acland Hood, which is situate on the shore of the Channel, and is a most picturesque and beautifully-arranged abode for anyone delighting in fine scenery. From thence the traveller should make his way through Watchet to the quaint old town of Dunster, where His Royal Highness the Prince of Wales recently took up his abode in the grand old castle, the property of Mr. Luttrell, who entertained the Prince and a numerous list of distinguished visitors during his brief stay in this portion of his dominions, where for the first time he enjoyed the exciting pastime of hunting the wild red-deer. After exhausting the wonders of Dunster, a visit should be paid to the Hill of Dunkerry, the highest point on the coast, on which stands the beacon that warns the mariner during his passage up and down Channel of the dangers of this rugged shore. From this elevated hill a grand view of the country in the vicinity of Exmoor is obtained, and will well repay the traveller for the trouble taken in exploring these lovely scenes; and he should make his way to Cloutsham Ball, the property of Sir Thomas Dyke Ackland, which he will find most beautifully placed amidst leafy combes, dense woodlands, and verdant vales. Then, returning to the coast, a pleasant journey brings the traveller to Minehead, and thence on to Porlock, at either of which places good hotels will be found. The view of Porlock Bay and the surrounding country is grand; and a visit to Hawkcombe Head will enable the visitor to see a large tract of this wild country. And from thence he can visit Oare Valley, Badgworthy Waters, and Doone Valley, and the romantic scenes amidst which "Lorna Doone" is supposed to have resided, as told in the popular novel bearing that title, in which an admirable description is given of the wild part of North Devon. Thence on by way of Culbone, Glenthorn, the Foreland, and Countisbury, to Lynmouth, following the coast-line all the way. After dwelling as long as time permits amongst the beauties of Lynton, making excursions inland to the many points of interest, then away by Trentishoe, Combmartin Bay, and Ilfracombe is reached. Here a long *séjour* may be made to great advantage, the surrounding country being exquisitely beautiful, as well as the sea-views. Here every accommodation will be found for the visitor, and the longer he protracts his stay, the greater will be his admiration of the scenery of both inland and seaboard. Should time permit the visit may be extended to Barnstaple and Bideford Bay, and Westward Ho. Then returning by railway from Barnstaple, passing by Swimbridge and South Molton, the traveller should halt at Dulverton; there he will find excellent accommodation and moderate charges at either the Lion or Lamb hotels. At the close of October the scenery will be found at its greatest beauty; the dense, many-coloured woods, the emerald-green valleys, the sparkling streamlets, the tall hills, the narrow lanes hemmed in with straggling hedges, and banks clothed with innumerable ferns of every description, all combine to make up a pleasing picture. Adjacent to Dulverton is Pixton Park, the seat of the Earl of Carnarvon, through whose park flows the river Barle, well-stocked with fine trout, and shaded by the splendid trees that overhang the stream. A walk through the park will enable the visitor to see some specimens of the finest beeches, horse-chestnuts, and limes, such as would delight the eye of an artist in search of the picturesque. A beautiful drive is that which leads past Hele Bridge along the Valley of the Exe, by Haddon Woods, and on towards King's Brompton. Another beautiful ride or walk is by the side of the brawling river Barle, and along the valley that leads to Withypool. In the vicinity of Hawkridge the scenery is truly beautiful, and at Castle Bridge, where the waters of the Danes Brook meet and mingle with those of the Barle, the visitor may pause for awhile and contemplate the beauties of nature. Here, seated beneath the magnificent and widely-spreading beech, which throws its shade over part of two counties, and dips into three several parishes, he can watch the trout leap, startle the game, and, if he wanders amidst the heather, awaken the blackcock from his nest in the brown heather; and if good-fortune befalls him, he may happen on a noble stag or a sleek hind in the deep shade of the densely-wooded combes which slope down to the banks of the river. Within a short distance he would come upon Torr Steps—Druidical stepping-stones forming a bridge across a broad and deep bend of the river Barle; a romantic spot certainly, worthy of the special notice of painter, poet, and tourist, who may wander in many lands before they find so grand a piece of sylvan scenery. Another lovely drive may be had by traversing Winsford Hill, passing through Comber Gate and making for Exford. The entire length of this route is a grand and far-reaching panorama of undulating country, extending in one direction to Dartmoor, with hill and dale, meadow and moorland, densely-wooded combes and sparkling rivulets; whilst on the other side the view extends over the Brendon Hills to Nettlecombe, with the Quantox Hills in the far-off distance. Leaving Dulverton, the line of railway passes through or near to Morebath, Wiveliscombe, and Milverton, landing the traveller again at Taunton, from whence, supposing him to be desirous of reaching London, he can travel to Chard, and thence by the South-Western Railway, thus varying his route, passing through Yeovil, Templecombe, Gillingham, and Salisbury—a preferable journey to that of the Great Western line, the country traversed being far more picturesque than by way of Reading, Bristol, and Bridgewater.

CHAPTER XXV.

A WINTER FAIR AT BOULOGNE.

A WORSE fate may befall a man than that of finding himself located for a brief period during the early winter time at Boulogne. In order to thoroughly enjoy a few days at this pleasant watering-place, it is essential that the visitor should be utterly devoid of care; as, in the first place, if he has anything rankling in his breast, he will not rest well, for "Where care lodges, sleep will never lie." Neither must he have any remorseful recollections; his conscience must be void of offence, for in such case he will not be in a fitting condition to fully enjoy a week's idling at Boulogne. Neither must he be impecunious, for, though a moderately-filled purse will suffice for his necessities, yet by having a few spare napoleons in his pocket he will be able to indulge in sundry *petits plaisirs*, to very great advantage. It is essential, moreover, that the idler should be of a cheerful disposition, looking on the bright side of things in general, and must in no case be what is called *blasé*, but must have yet some of the fire of youth remaining, in order to thoroughly enjoy a few days' active idleness, and duly appreciate and enjoy the exciting pleasures of the "Foire de St. Martin." Then it will greatly add to his comfort should he be the guest of an old friend—say in the Hauteville for choice; in whose well-ordered establishment there is profuse hospitality—a *très bonne cuisine*, wines of the country at discretion ("the claret smooth, red as the lip we press in sparkling fancy, while we drain the bowl; the mellow-tasted Burgundy; and, swift as the wit it gives, the gay champagne," to quote Thomson), and all the accessories which are found in the elegant home of an accomplished and lettered hostess, whose recollections of men and manners extend over a long period in the far-off days when George the Fourth was king; and he will have a fair chance of enjoying an exceedingly good time of it. Such were the conditions, at any rate, under which I passed a week of indolent enjoyment, amidst delightful society, loitering on the pier, watching the crews of the fishing-boats beating to windward in the teeth of a rattling north-easter, and breasting the waves that came rolling into the mouth of the harbour, whilst the sea-gull

> Claps the sleek white pinion to the breast,
> And in the restless ocean dips for rest;

or roaming leisurely along the streets, observing the display of wares in the numerous attractive and enticing shops; visiting the markets, especially the Halle au Poisson, in order to gaze upon the handsome *matelotes*, whose graceful figures are prominent amongst the inhabitants of the town; then, if tired of active exertion, lounging on a sofa surrounded with works of prose, poetry, and fiction, taking up by chance a volume of Russian poetry published more than half a century since, picking out such lines as these :

> Sporting like a happy child,
> Midst the forest's tenants wild.

Or :

> Sweetest, brightest rays of bliss,
> Never were as sweet as this.

Leading to the conclusion that the Russian of that period was not altogether a barbarian, the scratching of whose skin revealed the Tartar.

But what of the fair ? will be asked if I continue to deal with generalities. What of the fair ? forsooth! Why, a volume might readily be written of its numerous attractions. The site where it is held is the Haute ville, in front of the Palais de Justice, under the shadows of the Cathedral, and in the open space outside the gate, from which spot the best and most extensive view of the town, harbour, and coast is obtained, which, seen on a brilliant day, such as I was favoured with, formed a very pretty and pleasing picture—the brown sails of the innumerable fishing-boats being conspicuous far out to sea, whilst the white horses tumbled over one another, breaking with volumes of spray on the sandy and at times treacherous shore. By-the-way, the recent lamentable accident which caused the loss of the lives of three visitors, was, it appears to me, beyond doubt the result of a foolish disregard of repeated warnings; so they paid the penalty of their rash conduct, the sea being tremendously high, and the swirl of the tide sweeping them away remorselessly. With ordinary prudence the bathing at Boulogne is safe enough;

but if people will venture into the sea when the waves are running mountains high and the tide is rapidly receding, what other than a calamity such as that which so recently occurred is to be expected? Entering into the gay and festive scene, I observed innumerable stalls for the sale of cheap—I may say very cheap—jewellery, often exceedingly pretty in design; gaudily-painted vases, and china ornaments of every description, toys, bonbons, gingerbread, and pastry; and, above all, a *"Bazaar à vingt-cinq centimes,"* where everything, from curling-irons to resplendent articles of jewellery, may be purchased for that moderate sum. Then, passing through the gate, the fun of the fair commences, my attention being instantly attracted to the caravan of a somnambulist, and I read with much interest a placard announcing the fact that *"La critique est facile, l'art est difficile,"* with this remark: *" Si vous doubtez, veuillez entrer;"* but, not having the slightest doubt on the subject, I forbore to enter the somewhat frowsy-looking *salon*, preferring to admire the external exhibition rather than penetrate the hidden mysteries of the many shows assembled at the spot—for instance, the *Menagerie des Indes*, from which issued stupendous roars as of wild beasts in anger, but which I feel morally certain were only the hoarse brayings of a deep-toned brazen horn.

Great as is the excitement of the inhabitants by day, yet it is by night that the acme of enjoyment is reached. Then the tinkling of bells, the deep tones of the gong, the sharp crack of the rifle, the glare of innumerable lights, and the hoarse tones of the showmen proclaim that the real fun of the fair has commenced. I watch the motley throng eagerly starting on the *voyage sans fin*, or, as we should describe it, riding on a "merry-go-round." There is the shoeless gamin, the staid middle-aged Frenchman, the *matelotes* and their admirers, the sailor and his lass, the *demoiselles de comptoir*, and the young men of the town, revolving round the gorgeously decorated and brilliantly lighted temple of pleasure, to the festive accompaniment of drum and organ, playing continuously the popular air of the "Jolie Parfumeuse," all for the small sum of one sous for the course, and a long course too.

> By sports like these are all their cares beguiled—
> The sports of children satisfy the child;

and why not ? I ask. Tempted by the title of one particular show, I resolved to witness the exhibition of *L'Enfer*, and, paying my *vingt-cinq centimes*, the price of admission to the first-class seats, with a feeling somewhat akin to awe, I lift the heavy curtain and enter the mysterious chamber, amidst a clash of cymbals, the roll of the drum, and the deep-toned notes of the organ, and, taking my seat in front of the proscenium, I read these startling words : "*A la plus grande gloire du Satan.*" The walls, the ceiling, the panels, are decorated with symbols more or less devilish in their designs. The people flock in, the house is crowded, the curtain draws up, and you behold Satan reviewing the army of *âmes condamnées*, who, having crossed the Styx, are relegated to the cavernous depths below, amidst the beating of the gong, the rattle of the drum, and the explanatory remarks of the showman. First to appear on the scene was the *avocat*, whose manner of life was

described as having been somewhat shady, so to speak;
he is hastily disposed of, amidst the derisive shouts of
the audience, and the vivid flame of some fulminating
material which adds solemnity to the scene. Then
follows the *boulanger* who has been selling inferior
bread, the butcher convicted of short weight, the tailor
addicted to cabbage, the drunkard who has passed his
days at *L'Assommoir*, who, when consigned to the
shades below, goes off with a bang and an amount of
blue light that is a moral in itself; the curé who has
disgraced his religion, the lady of fashion who has
degraded her order—all these puppets being introduced by a marvellously clever little devil, himself a
puppet too, whose antics delighted the beholders
beyond measure. Then came what I suppose was an
allegorical piece of business, Time rowing Cupid across
the Styx; but in an instant the proceeding is reversed,
and Time is rowed back with haste. I presume this
meant that the blind god is not to be got rid of even
by Time, being immortal, as we have always understood him to be. Whether or no such an exhibition
is moral, and calculated to improve the mind, I decline
to say; but at any rate it was very droll indeed.

After this, attracted by a very clever wind-inflated
figure of Punch, I paid my two sous and entered in.
This was a somewhat disappointing exhibition, consisting of three dozen monkeys of different sizes,
passing through a doll's house, on which was written
"*Hôtel des Singes*,".or huddling and gibbering in the
corner.

After this I was specially attracted by a show
entitled "*Le Bagne.*" In the front were two life-sized
automatic figures, representing convicts, clothed in the

prison garb, monotonously grinding the air, representing the *travaux forcés* of the *Bagne*; whilst the face of one hideous criminal peeped through the iron bars, moving his mouth mechanically. Then I entered this veritable chamber of horrors, amidst the fanfare of trumpets, the rattle of drums, and the peals of the rich-toned hand-organ. In this exhibition I was again doomed to be disappointed—it was all glare, glitter, tinsel, and horror outside; but within it was merely a representation by puppets, moving mechanically, showing life in a prison. Then followed games of chance, and I plunged into tombolas, lotteries, and drawings for prizes madly, though never staking more than two sous at a time, and rarely winning one of the many glittering prizes offered to the gamester. More fortunate were the *matelotes*, who bore off gilded vases, figures of shepherds and shepherdesses, packets of bonbons, toys, or whatever fell to their lot. All was mirth, joviality, good-temper, and pleasantry; not a harsh word or coarse expression, and, above all, not a sign of intoxication amongst the many revellers at the Foire de St. Martin. A great desire being evinced on the part of two of the ladies who were idling at Boulogne to be photographed in the costume of the *matelotes*—a thing which is of daily occurrence when the town is thronged with visitors—we proceeded to the home, in the Quartier de la Marine, of the once famous Caroline, *La Belle Ecaillère*, and Queen of the Halle au Poisson, in order to borrow costumes for the occasion. Entering into the beautifully kept house, we were met by the granddaughter of the noted beauty of bygone days—a lovely girl of sweet seventeen, fair, with light-brown wavy hair, blue eyes, an exquisite figure, and small, beautifully-shaped hands and feet, after the fashion of *matelotes* in general, who are remarkable for those essentials to beauty of form. The costume of this fascinating demoiselle was, as well as I can describe it, composed of a brown jacket (showing her graceful figure to the greatest advantage), a corsage, gray shawl artistically arranged, a red petticoat with a blue tablier, gray worsted stockings, and *patins*, or wooden shoes. The walls were decorated with pictures; on the mantelshelf were the figure of the Virgin and a cross; on the chest of drawers a group of artificial flowers; and in one corner of the room the state-bed, with its blue curtains lined with lace, and a snow-white covering, not by any means for use, being little more than three feet in length, but an essential article of furniture in all houses of this class. With the greatest courtesy and kindness, not only the requisite articles of costume were offered, but the massive golden earrings and chains were most readily lent—articles of jewellery which always form conspicuous ornaments on the persons of *les belles matelotes*.

CHAPTER XXVI.

PICCADILLY.

" FLED now the sullen murmurs of the North,
   The splendid raiment of the Spring peeps forth,"

Was the observant remark of the "Farmer's Boy" in the good old times when seasons came in regular rotation, and things atmospheric were much less mixed up than they are nowadays. For the last two or even three years the "Rosy-bosomed Spring," the beauties of which were the theme of the poet and the study of the painter, and whose advent was ushered in with garlands gay and posies gathered in the woodlands wild, on the first day of the "merrie month of May," was, to speak in racing parlance, "nowhere." It was not merely a case of "Winter lingering in the lap of Spring," for in truth it fairly sat down upon it, and the result was disastrous in the extreme.

The meets of the Four-in-Hand and Coaching Clubs, the pleasant gatherings at Sandown, the Orleans and Ranelagh Clubs, the aristocratic meetings at Hurlingham, the enjoyable rides "down the road" on the well-appointed modern stage-coaches, polo, cricket-matches, lawn-tennis parties, all were signal failures, and the result vanity and vexation of spirit.

Never a rift in the clouds was observed, not a gleam of sunshine to gladden the heart; how then was it possible for the youthful beauty, looking forward to a successful *début*, to exhibit her unrivalled figure, exquisitely designed costume, and faultless *chaussure* to advantage, when what should have been velvet lawns were stagnant swamps, and leafy groves but damp and dripping woods? whilst the ceaseless patter of the envious rain compelled even the bravest wearer of the most lovely and irreproachable toilet to conceal its beauties within the folds of a comfortable but ungraceful ulster.

However, in this year of grace a somewhat better state of things prevails, for at length we are favoured with sunshine and fair weather, and the business of the season commences in earnest. Desiring to survey mankind, not from China to Peru, but over the more limited area extending from Piccadilly to the Park—where, by-the-way, you will see many more of the notable personages of the world than you would in the more widely extended prospect—I proceeded at an early hour of the morning to the Bath Hotel, Piccadilly, which admirable and pleasant hostelry is well known to a number of our country squires, who year after year locate themselves in the comfortable establishment at the corner of Arlington Street, the pivot on which the world—the fashionable world, I mean—revolves, and, seated at the commanding windows of the hotel, see a vast deal of life without any undue exertion. Previously to crossing over to the noted White Horse Cellars, for the purpose of witnessing the departure of the stage-coaches of the period, which start from thence daily on their admirably selected routes, it was advisable to order breakfast—an important measure—for unless you commence the day well, how can you expect to conclude it satisfactorily? " Waiter! cutlets of Severn salmon plain, slices of ham carefully broiled, plovers' eggs, coffee and curacoa at 11.30." "Yes, sir! Anything more, sir?" "No—that is to say, you may throw in a leg of a spring chicken—devilled, of course." "Yes, sir! any wine, sir?" and that question set me thinking—there are some people who hold that the proper time to take champagne is midday. I would not for the world attempt to bias others by giving an opinion, and I prefer leaving the matter to local option, lest I should appear to be interfering with freedom of opinion. "Well, yes," was my reply, "a bottle of old Pommery—the same as I had at dinner the other day." Then the cheery winding of a well-blown horn announced the coming of the Windsor coach, which starts at 10.30 daily (Sundays excepted) from Hatchett's, travelling *viâ* Richmond, Twickenham, Hampton Court, over Staines Bridge, to the well-known White Hart Hotel. Weather permitting, this coach invariably starts with a good load, and is admirably horsed, as well as cleverly, carefully, and punctually tooled over the pleasant line of road, by its experienced proprietor, Mr. H. Bailey, by whose side I have enjoyed an agreeable ride on several occasions. Having taken up its load, the Windsor coach moves off, and quickly disappears down Piccadilly. By this time there is a crowd of lookers-on assembled to witness the coming and going of the stages—some mere idlers, some old, time-worn, horsey-looking men, whose apparel oft proclaims the man to have been at one time or other connected with the road. Then you may observe

some of the staunch supporters of coaching, such as
Colonel Tyrrwhit, Sir Henry de Bathe, Major Dixon,
Captain Hargreaves, Dr. Hurman, etc., and some
would-be patrons of the art of coachmanship, who
assume a knowledge if they have it not. Then follows
the "Old Times," described in the advertisements as
being a fast four-horse coach, running all the year
round to Virginia Water, by way of Richmond, Bushey
Park, Hampton, Shepperton, and Chertsey, starting
at 10.45 A.M., and arriving at 1.30 P.M., leaving again
at 3.40 P.M., thus allowing a little over two hours for
a capital luncheon at The Wheatsheaf, and a saunter
amidst the pleasant scenery in the vicinity. This day
the coach is worked by "Selby," whose skill as a
workman on the bench stands in high repute. After
the departure of the "Old Times," the enlivening
tones of the horn are again heard, and from different
directions are seen approaching the "New Times," of
which Mr. Walter Shoolbred is now the sole proprietor,
and the "Defiance," the property of Mr. Carleton
Blythe, and worked solely by him throughout the
whole of the long journey—*viâ* Tunbridge Wells to
Brighton. This, though a large venture, requiring
over sixty horses to cover the ground extending over
a distance of $72\frac{1}{2}$ miles, is nothing to his performance
of last year, when he worked his coach from Oxford,
through London, to Cambridge, making 120 miles in
all. Admirably appointed, capitally horsed, and well
coached by the proprietor, assisted by Fownes, is the
"Defiance," and it starts from Hatchett's sharp to
time, the four spicy chestnuts going merrily along
Piccadilly on its downward journey. The "New
Times," which does the pleasant journey through a

beautiful line of country to Guildford, is also an admirably appointed coach, capitally turned out, well horsed, and driven in first-rate style, with the strictest attention to punctuality, by its clever coachman, Mr. Shoolbred. The coaches running from The Cellars are fewer than usual this year. No doubt the dismal seasons of the past two or three years discouraged the proprietors, who found small returns and little profit in the wet times they experienced, and it is to be feared that when the well-known Messrs. Banks have made up the books the balance will be found on the wrong side. As there was nothing more to be seen until 5 o'clock, when Mr. Robinson's coach leaves for Thames Ditton and Chertsey—a journey which I strongly recommend to anyone who wishes to enjoy a good time and to travel in first-rate style over a pleasant road, passing through Kew, Richmond, and Bushey Park—then to breakfast with what appetite we may; after which, lighting a cigar and reclining in a comfortable armchair, I note from the windows of these apartments a host of performers in the lively drama of life; with

> Pride in their port, defiance in their eye,
> I see the lords of human kind pass by,

to use Goldsmith's well-known lines; and, what interests me far more, many a lady fair, concerning whom the poet observes,

> As for the women, though we scorn and flout 'em,
> We may live with, but cannot live without 'em.

Well, I think Dryden was right when he enunciated that opinion, for undoubtedly it would have been a trifle dull had not Eve and her descendants appeared on the stage to play the rôle of companions in our hours of ease, and ministering angels at appropriate times and seasons.

Then crossing over from Charles Street, I see that kindly and popular peer, Lord Rowton, whose honours, so well deserved and gracefully bestowed, not even the most envious of his opponents can begrudge, for it may be said with truth, "Nothing becomes him ill that he would well." Then passes Lord Cork, whose reappointment as Master of the Buckhounds will be hailed with delight by many who hunt with the "Queen's;" and though his ways—political, I mean —are not my ways, yet I will willingly follow so genial a leader when he goes a rattler across a good line of country at the tail of the Royal Hounds. Then next passes a thoroughly well-appointed brougham, drawn by a pair of stylish, high-stepping horses, driven by the stateliest of coachmen, who is conveying one of the house of Rothschild to the City, not on pleasure, but on business bent. When I see that grave retainer going on his daily journey eastward, I always imagine that during the interval between his arrival and departure he fills some high fiduciary post in that wonderful establishment, so thoroughly business-like and reliable does he look. By-the-way, he once did me a service unwittingly, for, having occasion to meet "a party in the City" in reference to a monetary arrangement—a bill at three months, if my memory serves me—I passed down St. Swithin's Lane when this equipage was standing at the corner of New Court, and being recognised by the staid charioteer with a respectful touch of his hat, my capitalist, who up to this time had appeared somewhat indisposed to entertain my proposition, at once, on witnessing the recognition, fell in with my views, and passing into his office quickly drew upon me; I promptly accepted; a friend, merely as a matter of form, "jumped up behind," then there was at once a mercantile and negotiable instrument which, if I remember rightly, was not provided for when it came to maturity, and consequently had to be renewed. Leisurely passing along Piccadilly I see the member for Brecknock, and the constituency of this borough are to be congratulated at having secured so thorough a gentleman as Mr. Cyril Flower to represent them in Parliament. Then going in the direction of Apsley House I observe a park-phaeton, drawn by two matchless black cobs, with grand action, and in blooming condition, marvellously well driven by a young lady, whose radiant face beams with pleasure and delight as she threads her way confidently through the crowd of vehicles; the servant who sits behind appearing to be fully impressed with the responsibility of being entrusted with the care of the hope and the pride of the family he serves. By this time I had finished my cigar; and speaking of smoking reminds me of an anecdote of Keeley, whom I met at a garden-party at the close of his career. Having been requested by our host to ascertain if he had everything he required, I asked amongst other questions whether he had a good cigar.

"Yes, sir," he replied, "I have got a good cigar, but it has got one fault."

"Pray tell me what it is," I said, "that I may rectify it."

"It is too short, sir, too short," was his prompt reply.

Then my hack being announced, I mounted and rode down Piccadilly to the Park, to continue my observation of men and manners, for in that fashionable resort all classes are to be seen—

From thoughtless youth to ruminating age.

CHAPTER XXVII.

THE PARK.

Now that we have received a long overdue instalment of summer weather, an opportunity has been afforded of viewing Hyde Park to the greatest advantage. Many and great have been the improvements effected in the metropolis, but none equal the alterations that have been made in the parks, by planting and beautifying what were barren common-like lands, and converting them into trimly-kept pleasure-grounds, gay with parterres of lovely flowers, blossoming shrubs, and smooth velvety lawns. Entering the Park a few days since, I found the rhododendrons, azaleas, and other beautiful shrubs in full bloom, and I said to myself:

> Who can paint
> Like Nature? Can imagination boast,
> Amidst its gay creation, hues like hers?
> Or can it mix them with that matchless skill,
> And lose them in each other, as appears
> In every bud that blows? If fancy then
> Unequal fails beneath the pleasing task,
> Ah! what shall language do!

The day was lovely, and a host of gaily-dressed ladies were promenading beneath the shades of the spreading elms; whilst others more or less well-mounted were in the Row. Drawn up in a line were many personages well known in society, in barouches, park-phaetons, and victorias. There is Mrs. Cornwallis West, accompanied by her children, her carriage being surrounded by a host of admirers; then Colonel Ewart's coach, drawn by four good-looking chestnuts, pulls up at the top of the Row; and many others in vehicles of different descriptions are seen watching the throng of pedestrians and riders. Now passes quietly along H.R.H. the Prince of Wales, followed by a well-mounted groom, attracting no more attention than would have been accorded to any gentleman of distinction when riding in this fashionable resort. Then follows Lord Calthorpe on the magnificent chestnut horse recently purchased, at a fabulous price, of Mr. S. Sheward, who had intended to have kept him for his own use; next comes Colonel Vyvian, also on a very handsome high-bred chestnut—and it is even betting as to which of the two grand animals—Lord Calthorpe's or that which the Colonel bestrides—is the best, though as to action and style of going, I give the preference to his lordship's recent purchase. Next comes "a bevy of fair women," conspicuous amongst whom I notice Mrs. Lawson, mounted on her beautiful, dark chestnut, thorough-bred horse. High-couraged, but having a good temper, he is the proper form of horse to carry so good a rider. Accompanying Mrs. Lawson is her daughter, mounted upon her favourite roan cob, one of the best-made animals of his class I have ever seen, being marvellously well-shaped, and having high courage, capital action, and good manners. Cantering quietly along is Miss Wylie, also on a chestnut, which she rides in good style, for she is an excellent horsewoman, with, as one can easily see, an exceptionally light hand. Then I note Mrs. Pritchard Rayner, a lady whom I have noticed on many occasions going right well with the Atherston and North Warwickshire hounds; Mrs. Langtry, looking exceedingly well as she steers her handsome nag along the Row; the Countess of Lonsdale, the justly observed of all observers, mounted upon the handsome brown horse which I think is the same that carried her so brilliantly with the Cottesmore and the Quorn; the Hon. Hugh Lowther, riding "Mohican," with which he took a prize at the Agricultural Hall, a thoroughbred who has been taught to perform properly by this bold and skilful horseman.

Of the costumes of those promenading on this occasion by the side of the Row, much might be said by one acquainted with millinery and the many devices designed to increase the attractions of the human form divine. To my untutored eyes the attire of the many passing by resembled the ever-changing views seen in a kaleidoscope, so bright and varied were the hues of their garments. Two or three striking dresses, however, I could not fail to notice. One of black satin, worn by a beautiful girl, with black hair and eyes to match, and of a figure that any sculptor would have given the world to copy, a specimen, in truth, of an English maiden of high degree, one almost

Too fair to worship; too divine to love.

Another, consisting of a crimson velvet tight-fitting jacket, with a silken skirt of a less pronounced colour, was graced by a fair girl of superb figure, lovely complexion, soft brown hair, and brilliant brown eyes, which told of mirth and light-heartedness; somewhat a trying style of dress if worn by any other than a thoroughly ladylike and graceful woman. Another fascinating maiden was habited in a costume of dark brown velvet, wearing a Gloire de Dijon rose as a contrast. Another lady in black silk costume with beaded *passementerie* and cape, relieved by a poppy, worn at the throat, according to the prevailing fashion, attracted attention, as did one in deep heliotrope velvet, with hood and bonnet of a pale shade. So much for the costumes of the period, which certainly are somewhat startling, and not always in the good taste of those described. A custom more honoured in the breach than in the observance, by-the-way, is, I am happy to say, evidently falling into desuetude; I allude to the fashion which prevailed for a time of dyeing the hair what by courtesy was called a golden hue, but which I should describe as gamboge—one in my opinion of the least fascinating of the many alluring and seductive baits which our would-be enslavers ever employed, for though

> Fair tresses man's imperial race ensnare,
> And beauty draws us with a single hair,

that hair-line must be a natural and not an artificial one if it is to land a big fish. Henceforth I trust that this meretricious style of embellishment will be confined to the ballet-dancers of minor theatres; for though nothing can possibly be more beautiful than auburn hair, especially when streaked with threads of gold, or that of a pure golden hue, it is essential that the complexion should be in complete harmony with the colour of the locks; therefore I say, above all things be natural, for Nature will not allow liberties to be taken with her with impunity, and by going in opposition to her laws, that will be found to be a delusion which was intended for a snare.

Certainly in no other city in the world will you see such a number of handsome equipages and noble horses as are to be found in Hyde Park, at the height of the season. For instance, the phaeton and pair of gray and bay handsome high-stepping horses, which savour strongly of Green Street, the property of Mr. Arthur Anderson; the well-appointed buggy of Captain Selwyn, of the Blues, drawn by a sensational stepper, considered by many people to be the grandest goer in London at the present time; the phaeton of Mr. Emile Levitas, with his remarkably handsome brown horses; Lord Lismore's neat brougham and splendid chestnut horse; Lord Fife's handsome team; Mr. Blundell Leigh's buggy and high-class horse; Sir William Eden's coach and four topping nags; Count Munster's drag and spicy chestnuts; Sir Thomas Peyton's workmanlike team; Lord Calthorpe's splendid cab and grand horse, certainly one of the best equipages to be seen. This is, I think, one of the pleasantest vehicles for London work, infinitely superior to the now popular buggy, but it must be first-rate; the horse high-couraged, a grand stepper, resolute but temperate, the cab of the best style, and the tiger smart, handy, and irreproachably dressed—and as his lordship spares no expense, and possesses excellent taste and judgment it is no wonder that he has the best of everything, notably his handsome, shapely, high-stepping cob, a model animal.

But where there are so many magnificent equipages, it appears invidious to particularise, and, therefore, I recommend my readers to pay a visit to Hyde Park on a fine summer's day, from 12 to 2 o'clock in the morning. An opportunity is then afforded of hearing the band of the Blues, which daily discourses a beautiful selection of music at that time in front of the new barracks, a building, by-the-way, much better than the old, forming an ornament to the Park, and being far more convenient and comfortable for both officers and men.

Should the day be sultry, 6 o'clock in the evening is the time for a ride in the Row. The company will be more select, if less numerous, than in the morning, and the best-known personages of London society may usually be found.

CHAPTER XXVIII.

DOWN IN DENSHIRE.*

COME haste with me to Denshire, where the red-deer roams at will,
O'er the purple-bosomed moorland and the densely-wooded hill,
Through the valleys robed in verdure, rich as emeralds in their sheen,
Where the streamlet wanders swiftly, through the woodland wild and green,
Where the heather blooms so bravely, and tall birch-trees wave around,
Midst countless ferns so beautiful, that densely clothe the ground,
Where woodbine sweet, and ivy green, their tendrils fondly twine
Round mountain-ash and hazel bough, where blooms the eglantine;
Where the foxglove in its glory midst the bracken rears its head,
Beneath the grand old beech-tree, with branches widely spread.

* Denshire is the old English name for Devonshire.

'Tis there at dawn of morning, in the autumn of the year,*
We'll rove the woodlands gaily to track the wild red-deer.
Then fleetly o'er the heather, through many a sparkling rill,
Along the verdant valleys, o'er moorland, dale, and hill,
We'll chase our antlered quarry, whilst each covert shall resound
With the halloo of the huntsman and the deep note of the hound,
Whilst every hill shall echo, and re-echo back again,
The music of the cheery horn o'er all the wide-spread plain;
Then on we'll urge our flagging steeds, and still our spurs we'll ply—
The die is cast, his doom is sealed—"This day a stag must die."

* Stag-hunting in Devonshire commences on August 12th.

CHAPTER XXIX.

LINES

SUGGESTED by a visit to Jack Babbage, aged eighty years, formerly the noted huntsman of the Devon and Somerset Staghounds, and his "auld wife," Jean, now pensioners, spending the evening of their days on the estate of J. Froude Bellew, Esq., at Rhyll, in close vicinity to the wild heather-clad range of hills known as Hawkridge.

> The stars shone bright
> That lovely night,
> When roaming through the heather;
> We, nothing loath,
> Then plighted troth,
> To live and love together.
>
> Now many a day
> Has passed away
> Since first in summer weather,
> Through emerald glade
> And woodland shade,
> We loitered in the heather.

*   *   *   *

Ah, dearest Jean,
We once again
Are tottering through the heather;
The storms of life,
The world's fierce strife,
We long have braved together.

But on we'll go,
Come weal or woe,
Linked yet by love together;
Still true and fast,
Whilst life shall last,
Amidst the faded heather.

CHAPTER XXX.

THE OLD SPORTSMAN'S LAMENT.

Dolefully, drearily, dismally dull,
With sorrow and sadness my cup is brimful,
Old age has crept o'er me, my best time is past,
Where once I was first now I'm doomed to be last;
But grunting and grumbling the matter won't mend,
And sooner or later all pleasures must end.
  Then, ho! for a flagon, and quick pass it round,
  To the health of the huntsman, the horse, and the hound!

Come fill up the flagon, and pledge me with zest,
As we sing of the run of the season—the best;
How Gaylass and Ruby stooped well to the scent,
And away o'er the pastures so merrily went.
When a certain bold rider, of sportsmen the chief,
O'er those stiff posts and rails came "so muchly" to grief.
  Then, ho! for a flagon, etc.

Let us hunt with the Cottesmore, from Ranksboro' Gorse,
With the Belvoir from Croxton (in fancy, of course);

With the Quorn let us gallop from famed Kirby Gate,
And climb Burrow Hills at a heartbreaking rate;
O'er yonder big fields where the Whissendine flows,
Let us follow Tom Firr, as "Yoi, over," he goes.
   Then fill up the flagon, etc.

Let us ride with the Pytchley, whilst to Goodall we stick,
As he shows us the way in a fast run from Crick,
Where the fences are large, and the pace oft's severe
(Unless you've a stout nag you've no business there).
If mounted by Darby, as I have been oft,
How grand is a gallop from famed Yelvertoft.
   Then fill up a flagon, etc.

With the stag-hounds in Essex let's follow the chase;
If you ride o'er the Roothings you must go the pace,
For the country is open, the ditches are wide,
And it takes a bold horse to do them in his stride;
If nervous, or timid, or fearful to fall,
Don't follow H. Petre or Collinson Hall.
   Then, ho! for a flagon, etc.

Then away with dull care, let's be gay to the last,
Why sorrow or fret o'er the time that is past;
Remember those lines in which Horace did say,
"What has been, has been," and each one has his day.
Let us dwell on the past, then, with pleasure, not pain,
And in mem'ry live o'er the old times again.
   Then, ho! for a flagon, etc.

CHAPTER XXXI.

THE HIGHLANDS.

I.

Upon the Grampian Hills entranced I stand,
Gazing with rapture on the weird highland,
Moorland and mountain, countless rippling rills,
Springing impatient from the heath-clad hills,
Leaping from ledge to ledge they downward flow,
Murmuring soft music as they fall below;
Onward through correis wild they glide
In headlong haste to swell the river's tide.
All, all is solitude and silence there.
Mark yon grand eagle hovering high in air!
The careful shepherd, as he tends his flocks,
Wrapped in his plaid, reclines amidst the rocks;
His watchful eye the bird of prey descries,
Arising promptly, off the marauder flies,
Upwards he mounts, baulked of his helpless prey,
Circles around, then swiftly sails away,
Adown the glen, far o'er the topmost height,
Higher and higher until lost to sight.

II.

Along Glentaitneach* idly let me stray,
In sunshine bright on glorious autumn day,
Adown "The Pleasant Glen;" a toilsome walk I ween,
Where midst the mountains nestles Loch Na-Nean.
Rough is the road and steep the mountainside,
Down which the babbling waters swiftly glide,
On either side grim Grampians cast their shade
O'er the bright waters flowing down the glade;
Whilst springing forth from grandest of them all,
Downward descends the noisy waterfall.
Far, far away, the "Muckle Hull" is seen,
Surmounting which, you gaze on Loch Na-Nean.
'Tis there the sportsman long ere breaks the day,
With stealthy step in silence wends his way;
Onward he toils for many long hours, and then
Sees within range the antlered monarch of the glen.
With fatal aim, swiftly his bullet flies,
And on his native heath the red-deer, falling, dies.

III.

There, midst tall mountains, boldest of them all,
In fair Glen Beg, admire the grim Cairnwall;
Note well its grandeur, and its summit scan,
Where midst gray boulders thrive the ptarmigan.
Upwards ascend, scaling its stony height,
And gaze with pleasure on the glorious sight
Which meets the eyes whichever way they turn—
Loch, moor, and mountain, heather, rill, and burn.
Lovely Rhidorach, when I sing thy praise
'Tis in remembrance of those jovial days,

* Glentaitneach, or The Pleasant Glen.

When, gun in hand, we strove the grouse to kill
In correis wild, on many a heath-clad hill.
Steady stands Flora—up then the covey flies,
And quick on the ground the " brown bird " fluttering lies.
Now, rod in hand, by river's bank we stray,
Just ere the shades of night o'ertake the day;
With cunning hook and small deceptive fly,
For speckled trout in likely pools we try;
With practised hand we ply the rod and reel,
Homewards returning with a well-filled creel.

CHAPTER XXXII.

DRIVING RED-DEER.

"Essex," says Camden, writing the history of that county, in days long past, " is a country large in compasse, fruitful, full of woods, plentiful of saffron, and very wealthy; encircled as it were, on the one side with the maine sea, on the other with fish-full rivers." From time immemorial this, my native county, has been noted for sport of every description, for history tells us how "that simple saint, Edward the Confessor," granted a charter to Ranulph Peperking, of the Hundred of Chelmer and Dancing.

It was, then, with mingled anticipations and retrospects that I repaired, a few days since, to Thorndon Hall, near Brentwood, the seat of Lord Petre, in order to join in the sport of driving red-deer, his lordship having determined to do away with the herds of fallow and red deer which have so long roamed over the grand old park. At one period the herd consisted of somewhere about 2000 of these graceful animals, who rested beneath the shade of the countless oaks, or cropped the herbage in the verdant glades, and, when disturbed, disappearing amidst the luxuriant ferns, startling the pheasants, causing the rabbits to scuttle into their holes, and the chattering jay to give his loud note of warning that an enemy was invading their privacy. When I left London the ground was iron-bound in the grasp of a hard frost, which looked very like spoiling the sport in which I was to join; however, by noon a thaw had set in, and dull gray clouds overhung the wild common on which stands the extensive range of buildings, possibly very comfortable, but certainly far from picturesque, known as Warley Barracks.

Passing by this uninteresting specimen of modern architecture, I speedily arrived at the Lion Gate, and entered the precincts of the lordly domain so long the abode of the Petres. As I wended my way in the direction of the hall, I could not fail to note the difference in the appearance of the park nowadays as contrasted with what I remember as a boy, some half century or more since, when I rode side by side with the then Lord and Lady Petre, in pursuit of a gallant old fox, which we had found in the Warley Woods, at the tail of one of the finest packs of foxhounds ever maintained in the county of Essex. Then the music of the hounds in full cry, the sharp note of the huntsman's horn, the crash of the many well-mounted and hard-riding men who followed this crack pack, awoke the echoes, driving the startled deer into the inmost recesses of the covert, as we ran at a rasping pace through the densely wooded portions of the park, forcing Reynard at last to face the open and trust to speed to out-distance his pursuers. Now all was dull and drear, not a sound was to be heard, not a soul to be seen. The ground was strewed with withered leaves and broken branches, borne down by the heavy fall of snow, which did so vast an amount of damage to the trees, then covered with leaves, during the storm in the early days of October. At length the façade of the old hall became visible; no liveried lacqueys lounge at the doors, no prancing palfreys emerge from the large range of stabling; all is desolation, for nearly the whole of the large pile of building was destroyed by fire a year or two back, and the gaunt, blackened, massive walls plainly tell the tale of destruction.

Turning away from the dilapidated edifice, I went in search of the hunters, whose business it was that day to take the remainder of the herd of red-deer, many having already been captured, and the finest specimens sent to Weald Hall Park, the property of Mr. Christopher I. H. Tower, a thorough sportsman. Transferred to his beautiful park, with its splendid growth of fern, its grand old trees, undulating surface, extensive lake and lovely scenery, these noble animals will be a great addition to the already handsome, if somewhat limited, herd that roam at pleasure over the ancient domain which lies contiguous to Brentwood. Then, as I wended my way across the park, I heard in the distance the halloo of the hunters, evidently in pursuit of the game; and, suddenly emerging from the woodland, I see nine hinds and four stags. In an instant these beautiful creatures came to a halt on perceiving me, fearing doubtless that, though they had left the hunters far behind, they had fallen in with a fresh enemy. Remaining perfectly still, I watched with delight the movements of the little herd, which evidently were in doubt as to which way they should go to escape from their pursuers, finally moving off at a stately trot—the hinds leading the way, and the stags bringing up the rear; then, quickening their speed, they were soon lost to sight amidst the cover. Journeying along in the direction from which came the sounds that attracted my attention, I came upon a group of sportsmen, from whom I learnt that the hinds and stags, after being driven into the place where the nets were placed, had broken through the obstruction and escaped—only, as it proved, for awhile, for after a hasty luncheon we were speedily in pursuit again. By this time the rain began to descend steadily, whilst the wind howled through the leafless branches of the sturdy old oaks and chestnuts, this being varied with a smart storm of snow.

However, the work had to be finished, and the nets being spread along a considerable distance, the business of riding in the red-deer commenced in earnest. Led by Tiler, the stud-groom, who for many years has been in the service of Lord Petre, the horsemen were soon in pursuit of the deer, whilst a host of beaters were posted in different parts, to turn the hunted animals, and drive them in the direction of the spot where the stout nets were placed, the men holding themselves in readiness to secure the captives when the struggling animals became entangled in the snares spread for their capture. Loud halloos, the cracking of whips, and shouts of the beaters proclaim that the deer are being driven in the direction of the nets, and quickly the herd is discovered, bewildered and terrified by the noise of the riders who are in hot pursuit. For a moment they halt, finding enemies in front as well as eager pursuers in the rear; then suddenly they retrace their steps, dashing off at a tremendous speed, escaping for awhile, but only for awhile.

Tiler rides hard, a splendid horseman, urging on his well-bred steed, bent upon isolating some of the deer from the herd, knowing if they were all driven into the nets together, they would break down the barriers and escape. Then the loud and discordant shouts of the beaters announce that they are again in sight; this time the herd is divided, three stags and four hinds being separated from their fellows in adversity. Now they approach the spot where I had ensconced myself, with the view of witnessing the *dénoûment*. Louder and louder grow the shouts of the beaters and the halloos of the hunters, but once more the deer wheel round and dash back into cover. Again their relentless pursuers are on their track, and they are driven once more in the direction of the nets, the beaters closing around them. The eager horsemen gain ground upon them, it is in vain they try to head back; they are encompassed on all sides. Nothing is left for the panting animals but to dash at the nets, in the hope of thus escaping. Now is the hunter's moment of victory; a hideous uproar adds to the bewilderment of the fugitives, and they make a rush in a body at the nets. One noble old stag clears the net—which I measured subsequently, and found to be seven feet in height—and returns to the haunts in which he has so long dwelt undisturbed. But the remainder are entangled beyond hope of escape; the beaters throw themselves upon them. and, after a short struggle, the captive deer are bound and lie prostrate on the ground, though again and again they ineffectually struggled to get free. There lay a gray hind, which the keeper told me had led them many a mile at a rattling speed before she was taken; panting and distressed, terrified and bewildered, her beautiful eyes seemed to plead for release. Not so the fine young stag, who exerted all his strength to break his bonds, and finding his endeavours fruitless, bellowed loudly in hoarse complaining tones. Be it understood that there was no cruelty in the treatment of the deer, but one could not help feeling regret that, owing to the determination to break up the herd, it was necessary that they should be hunted from their accustomed haunts and deprived of their liberty, in order to carry out the decree which banishes these lordly animals from the soil on which they have so long flourished.

Time was now afforded to notice some of the sportsmen. There stood "Tom Mashiter" and his brother William, both well known with the stag, fox-hounds, and harriers of Essex, the former being a landed proprietor who has participated in every sport that this country could offer. I was reminded some fifty-three years since, that I had shown them a good run with the scratch pack with which, in our boyhood, we were wont to try our 'prentice hands at hunting, in and about the beautiful locality of Havering-atte-Bower, the spot selected by Edward the Confessor for a residence, where, however, history tells us his devotions were so greatly disturbed by the singing of countless nightingales that he prayed they might be prevented disturbing his meditations. History says that his prayer was granted, and never again was the "jug, jug, jug" of that sweet bird heard within the precincts of the park. In my time they abounded, and we, less devout than King Edward, rather liked them than otherwise. Next I see Mr. Collinson Hall, another good sportsman, well known throughout Essex, who, accompanied by Mrs. Hall, had come to see the last of the red-deer. Mr. Walker, the steward of the estate, and several gentlemen with whom I am unacquainted, also braved the inclement weather Once more the covert resounds with the loud halloos of the riders, the cracking of whips, the shouts of the beaters; then three stags and four hinds dashed up close to the nets, but, taking fright, they instantly wheeled round and rushed back. Their relentless pursuers were soon after them again, endeavouring to drive them into the nets, and once more they dashed up, halted suddenly, vainly endeavouring to find some mode of escape; then, terrified at the noise and the close approach of their foes, they made for the nets, and becoming speedily entangled in the meshes, in a few minutes, after some sharp struggles with their captors, they were bound in fetters, never again to roam the woodlands wild and verdant glades of Thorndon Hall.

CHAPTER XXXIII.

HUNTING IN ESSEX.

I ROSE on the occasion of a visit to Essex, to ascertain the state of the weather. When I withdrew the curtains and looked out upon the morn, the prospect was not encouraging. The wind moaned sadly through the bare leafless branches of the grand old elms, which were bending and swaying to the fitful blasts; whilst a flock of jackdaws, disturbed from their resting-place amidst the venerable branches, chattered noisily as they wheeled round and round, battling with the storm. The conclusion I came to was that there would be but little scent and poor sport if the gale continued its blustering throughout the day. The fixture of the "Essex Hounds," of which Sir Henry Selwin-Ibbetson is now the master, was Bentley Mill, close to the hospitable home of an old friend, who had invited me to ride with the stag and foxhounds over this sporting country, promising that I should be well mounted, an assurance that was highly satisfactory, as the fences are big, the ditches deep, and the banks tall and narrow, necessitating a clever steady horse, and a fairly good man, to live up to hounds through a clinking run of thirty-five minutes without a check, such as occurred during my visit. As we had only half a mile to go to cover, there was time after breakfast to look over the stables and farmsteads, and to examine the stables and live-stock; and it was satisfactory to note that as yet we are not entirely dependent upon foreign countries for our meat, as I saw a lot of West Highland bullocks of wonderful quality, which had been fatted and sold at a good profit, in order to supply some of the inhabitants of the metropolis with the roast beef of old England during the present Christmastide.

By this time the wind had dropped, and the weather was dry and pleasant; and mounting a five-year-old Lincolnshire mare, I accompanied my friend to the meet. On arriving at the four cross-roads adjacent to Bentley Mill, we found the Master had already put in an appearance, and a short time only elapsed before the huntsman, James Bailey, trotted up with the pack. Before the hounds were thrown into the adjoining cover, there was time to observe the "field." Among the number present I recognised Mr. Edward Ind, a stanch supporter of this hunt, accompanied by Miss Ind, and Lieutenant F. Ind, all mounted on good-looking nags; the Rev. Mr. Fane and Miss Fane, Colonel Howard, Mr. Harvey Foster, the secretary of the hunt, a light weight and hard-goer, whom it would be a difficult task to outpace when the fox, choosing a good line, gives a sharp half-hour over the cream of the country; Mr. Octavius Coope and Miss Coope, General Sir Lumley Graham, Mr. Walmsley, Mr. Collinson Hall, Mrs. Mackintosh of Havering, well mounted; Mr. and Mrs. R. Wood, on wheels, driving from point to point at a marvellous pace; Messrs. Sworder, Miles, Coleman, Pratt, Barber, etc. It was satisfactory to find that the tenant farmers of Essex were, even in these dismal times, represented by good men and true sportsmen.

So, moving off, we draw the Moors, a likely-looking covert, which, however, does not hold a fox to-day; then on to Gilstead Hall Covers, where we again fail to find. Next, we try Locksmith's Wood, but Reynard is from home on this occasion, though he was known to have been in the locality the previous day. Missing Weald Hall Park, which is a certain find, in consequence of Mr. Tower having fixed an early day to shoot his well-preserved covers, we draw unsuccessfully the Vicarage Woods and the Oaks. I attribute the scarcity of foxes in these well-known coverts to the fact of the crafty animals preferring the shelter of the dry hedgerows at this season, where they are less likely to be disturbed by the shooters and the rustling of the fallen leaves. Be that as it may, the same want of success attended our endeavours to find one of the vulpine race even in the extensive covers of Dagenham Park, though Bailey drew them thoroughly. Then we trotted off to Pirgo Park Wood, in which my far-dated experience of that well-known cover led me to the conclusion that we should not fail to find a fox, and a good one too. "Loo in, Loo in," "Halloo in," "Yoi, have at him there," cries Bailey. A hound speaks, then a musical chorus proclaims that we've found. "Hold hard!" cries Firr, the first whip; "let him have a chance to get away;" and at that moment I view a stout fox sloping off from the wood and going at full-speed over a large ploughed field in the direction of Curtice Mill Cover, whilst loud cries of " Tally ho!

tally ho!" proclaim that he is away. Then, galloping up comes the huntsman, who, with several twangs from his well-blown horn, brings up the eager hounds; the pack is laid on the line of the fox, and we go away at a merry pace. There is no shirking or craning at the fences, for, difficult as is this country, the riders with the Essex hounds are workmen, who come out to ride hard and go straight as a rule. Wide districts yet remain in Essex which have happily escaped the notice of the railway engineer and the speculative builder, both enemies of the worst order as respects fox-hunting. Although riding within thirty miles of the metropolis you will find as wild and sporting a country to go across as might be expected in the more distant parts of England. Quaint old farmhouses, approachable only by green lanes, large woodlands, wild pastures, venerable churches, brawling brooks without bridges, big fences, and wide ditches are the characteristics of this county. Those who have not a good eye, a light hand, strong nerves, and the knowledge how to pilot a clever horse over a difficult country should eschew Essex, and content themselves by riding over the downs in Sussex or the open country of Hampshire; for in this eastern district there is no help from macadam, no trusting to cutting in, no chance of making up on highways and byways the time lost by pottering or shirking a rasper. Unless you harden your heart and take the fences as they come, big or little as they may be, you will be nowhere at the end of a sharp burst. But whilst I am digressing the fox is running hard; and if the huntsman was present I should be soundly rated for babbling, a most reprehensible practice in his eyes, and " Forrard on, forrard on" would be his cry. Therefore I must proceed to tell how in due time I came up to a big fence with a narrow ditch, which, "if not as deep as a well or as wide as a church-door," yet was enough to have taken in both horse and rider. A gentle application of the rowels made my young mare go full tilt at the hedge and ditch, over which we landed in good form. Then on we gallop across Howletts Hall Farm, making straight for Navestock Park, pointing for Dudbrook, the seat of Lord Carlingford; but, turning sharp to the right, we gallop in the direction of Boys Hall Cover, then, bending to the left, go at a rattling pace over Lashes Farm, on to Ditchleys, leaving the Moors to the left, and making straight for Gilstead Hall Covers, finally running up to Weald Hall Park, where we lost our fox after a capital run of rather more than an hour. The ground rode well, the scent was good, and the pace lively enough for the most eager of sportsmen.

The kennels of the Essex hounds are situate at Harlow, and the country over which they hunt is very wide, extending across a large acreage of grass and ploughed lands around Harlow, Chelmsford, and Ongar, James Bailey, the huntsman, is a recent acquisition; and shows evident signs of being a workman, and has made a favourable impression on the members of the hunt. Sir H. Selwin-Ibbetson is very popular, and evinces every desire to show sport, hunting the country regularly four days a-week. Any real sportsman who may feel disposed to have a look at this useful pack will find ample accommodation at Brentwood, which is within half-an-hour's run from Liverpool Street by express trains, and will be rewarded by seeing excellent sport over a wild country.

On the following morning the fixture of the Essex Staghounds was Willingale, some three miles from Fyfield, in the Roothings of Essex, a wild open country admirably suited for stag-hunting. There is a wide expanse of light-riding land, with big ditches, on the one side of which grows a somewhat scrubby fence, and it requires a bold, resolute, well-bred horse to perform satisfactorily when hounds go the pace over this grand part of the county of Essex. The morning was wet and windy, but as my host had arranged to drive me to cover, the distance being thirteen miles, and his usual pace of travelling sixteen miles an hour, there was no occasion to hurry over the ample breakfast that was provided, and before we had finished that pleasant meal, the mist had cleared, and fair hunting weather prevailed through the remainder of the day. Vividly impressed on my mind was the rapid act of coachmanship I was doomed to endure throughout the whole journey to Willingdale. Up hill, down hill, on the level ground, round the sharpest of corners, we were whirled at the top speed of the blood-horse that drew the light well-balanced dogcart, into which I somewhat unwillingly mounted, for the behaviour of this light-hearted animal had reached my ears.

Pulling like a lion, and stepping in rare form, he flew through Kelvedon, away past Chipping Ongar, and laying hold of the bit in right earnest he dashed through Fyfield at the top of his speed, arriving in good time at the meet. With any other than the stalwart owner of this fiery steed I should have declined to ride; but the wonderful nerve and clever coachmanship of my companion reconciled me to my fate, though I admit to a certain amount of anxiety when I thought of the possibility of a buckle or a band breaking, and the probable result. On our arrival at the hospitable dwelling of the veteran, who for upwards of fifty years has ridden to hounds in this locality, we found breakfast awaiting, to which all-comers were invited by Mr. Richard Patmore and his son.

A few minutes only elapsed before the Hon. Henry W. Petre appeared on the scene with the pack. Dismounting, he joined the large party assembled around the table, many of whom had travelled long distances, finding their appetites sharpened by a quick gallop to the meet, and doing justice to the ample store of good things provided for the occasion. In this number of hard-riding sportsmen were to be found many noted performers, amongst whom were Mr. Charles Page Wood, Mr. Collinson Hall, Mr. Ralph Price, of Marshalls, near Romford, Dr. Bodkin, Messrs. Thomas Usborne, Colley, Percy Saunders, Harry Jones, James Christie, John Tabor, Rainer, Patmore, jun., Maddox, Corrie, Henry Garrett, Gibbon, and two gallant plungers from Colchester Barracks, etc.

As soon as breakfast was finished a hind was uncarted at the customary spot on the north side of the house, the usual law being allowed. Then the hounds being laid on to the line of the deer, quickly picking up the scent, go away at a splitting pace in the direction of the River Roden, but, turning sharp to the right, they make for Waples Mill, crossing the road, and bending sharp to the left, go at a racing pace in the direction of the King William publichouse, then, turning again to the left, they ran away in the direction of the Roden, which was crossed with considerable difficulty, the banks being steep and rotten.

Afterwards, leaving White Roothing Church on the right, they make for Mann Wood, passing through that cover on to Bury Wood, where the hind took to a piece of water on an adjoining farm, after a splitting run of thirty-five minutes without a check over this stiff country. After some delay, the quarry, having refreshed herself in the pool, emerged from her bath and went away again for twenty minutes, running a circle, and making for a farmstead, where she ought to have been taken, if it had not been for the apathy displayed by two or three horsemen, who seemed only to care for the gallop, taking no interest in the deer or the sport—a class of sportsmen whose room is better than their company. This was a bad compliment to a good master, and a word on the subject should be sufficient to put a stop to such malpractices, in the interest of legitimate riders. Finally, after running for some ten minutes longer, the hind was taken in the open, being, after some little trouble, secured and placed in safety. Thus ended one of the best runs of the present season. Amongst those in the first flight were the Master, Messrs. Collinson Hall, Tabor, Price, Colley, Usborne, Christie, Garrett, and the two officers from Colchester, who rode well throughout this clipping chase. Anyone who likes stag-hunting should try a day or two with Mr. Petre, and he will find, in my opinion, no better country than the Roothings.

During my visit to Dytchleys I had the opportunity of seeing the kennels and hounds of the Essex Union Foxhounds, and of being introduced to the new master, Mr. Carnegie, who hunts the pack himself, showing very good sport, notwithstanding his short knowledge of the locality. On arriving at Great Burstead, we found Mr. Carnegie at home. He had the hounds brought from the paddock, where they were being exercised, into the kennels for our inspection. A few minutes only elapsed before we recognised a thorough workman, equally at home in the field or the kennels, and it is evident that ere this season terminates there will be great improvements in this old-established pack. Mr. Carnegie brought from Scotland his hounds, horses, and servants; the old Union hounds are being drafted, many showing signs of wear and tear, and the infusion of new blood into this pack cannot fail to be satisfactory. A little time only is required for the new master to carry out his improvements. After inspecting the hounds we visited the stables, and saw an excellent string of useful, well-bred horses, good enough to go across any country; therefore, I think it may safely be said that the fortunes of the Essex Union are in the ascendant. The district over which they hunt is very large, extending from the River Thames to Chelmsford. Mr. Carnegie intends, I believe, to hunt the country four days a-week, and there is little doubt that, weather permitting, the members of this well-known hunt will find plenty of sport under the new management. Easily reached from London, those to whom it is inconvenient to travel long distances will be sure of sporting runs over a difficult country, with either the stag or fox hounds; and, provided the rider has his heart in the right place, is not afraid of a yawner, and has nags that are clever over tall banks and deep ditches, and at the same time are able to go the pace, he will never regret having located himself in the thoroughly sporting county of Essex.

THE END.

SPIERS & POND, LIMITED.

The Company's Principal Establishments in the Metropolis are—

The CRITERION, Piccadilly.

Luncheon served daily in the Grand Hall, from 12 till 3. **2s. 6d.** During the summer months.

The Table d'Hôte and Le Diner Parisien daily from 6 till 8; also on Sundays at 6.

Smoking Rooms, Lavatories, Ladies' Retiring Rooms, &c.

The GAIETY, Strand.

Table d'Hôte daily from 5.30 till 8 (Sundays excepted).

Commercial Dinner from 12 till 3.

Suppers in the Grill Room till midnight.

The HOLBORN VIADUCT HOTEL.

For Families and Gentlemen.

Also at all those **Railway Refreshment Rooms** *in London and throughout the Country where their Name is displayed.*

SPIERS & POND, Limited.

LONDON AND NORTH-WESTERN AND CALEDONIAN RAILWAYS.

WEST COAST (ROYAL MAIL) ROUTE
BETWEEN
ENGLAND AND SCOTLAND.

1st, 2nd, and 3rd CLASS TOURIST TICKETS, Available from the date of issue, up to and including the 31st December, 1882, are (during the Season commencing 1st May) issued from all Principal Stations in England to the chief places of interest in Scotland, and also from the same places in Scotland to English Stations.

Passengers by the Through Trains between **London (Euston Station) and Scotland** are conveyed in **Through Carriages** of the most improved description, and constructed specially for the accommodation of this Traffic.

SALOONS, FAMILY CARRIAGES, RESERVED COMPARTMENTS, and all other conveniences necessary to ensure comfort on the journey, can be arranged upon application to Mr. G. P. NEELE, Superintendent of the L. and N.-W. Line, Euston Station, London; Mr. IRVINE KEMPT, Caledonian Railway, Glasgow; or to any of the Station-masters at the Stations on the West Coast Route.

By the opening of the line of Railway from **CALLANDER to OBAN** Direct Railway Communication is now afforded by the West Coast Route to Loch Awe, Taynuilt, and Oban. Steamers sail in connection to and from Iona, Staffa, and the Western Islands.

TABLE OF EXPRESS TRAINS BETWEEN LONDON & SCOTLAND.

DOWN JOURNEY.

STATIONS.	Week Days.							Sundays.		
	a m	a m	a m	a m	p m	p m	p m	p m	p m	p m
London (Euston) . dep.	5 15	7 15	10 0	11 0	†8 0	8 50	9 0	8 0	8 50	0 0
Edinburgh (Princes St. Stn.) arr.	4 30	5 50	7 50	9 45	6 45	6 45	7 50	6 45	6 45	7 50
Glasgow (Central Station) . ,,	4 44	6 0	8 0	10 0	6 40	6 55	8 0	6 40	6 55	8 0
Greenock ,,	5 50	7 15	9 5	11 42	7 50	*7 50	*9 7	7 50	7 50	9 7
Stirling ,,	5 39	...	8 24	10 27	7 6	7 21	*8 43	7 6	7 21	8 43
Oban ,,	10 0	...	...	4 35	12 26	*12 55	...	12 26	12 55	...
Perth ,,	6 50	...	9 25	11 40	8 5	8 15	*9 55	8 5	8 15	9 55
Aberdeen ,,	10 10	...	...	3 20	11 40	11 40	*2 15	11 40	11 40	2 15
Inverness ,,	...	...	...	8 0	1 30	1 30	*6 25	1 30	1 30	6 25

UP JOURNEY.

STATIONS.	Week Days.						Sundays.	
	p m	a m	a m	a m	a m	p m	a m	a m
INVERNESS . . dep.	10 0	...	...	...	10 10	1 30	10 10	...
Aberdeen ,,	...	...	8.55	9 30	12 30	4 40	12 30	...
	a m		noon.					
Perth ,,	8 30	...	12 0	1 55	4 4	7 30	4 4	...
Oban ,,	5 30	...	8 0	...	12 40	3 55	...	...
Stirling ,,	9 30	...	1 5	3 24	5 3	8 30	5 3	...
Greenock ,,	9 0	...	1 10	3 0	5 0	8 10	...	...
Glasgow (Central Station) . ,,	10 0	10 30	2 15	4 20	6 0	9 15	6 0	9 15
Edinburgh (Princes St. Stn.) ,,	10 0	10 35	2 25	4 30	6 10	9 25	6 10	9 25
London (Euston) . arr.	8 0	10 5	4 30	5 30	4 5	8 0	4 5	8 15
	p m	p m	p m	a m	a m	a m	a m	a m

No connection from London to Places marked thus (*) on Saturday Nights.
† *Not run on Saturday night.*

THE LIMITED MAIL TRAINS

Travel by this route, and are in connection with the Mail Coaches to the Outlying Districts of the Highlands. These Trains have been accelerated between London and Edinburgh, Glasgow and Perth; and additional accommodation and increased facilities are now afforded to passengers travelling by them.

DAY SALOONS, with Lavatory Accommodation attached, are run between London and Edinburgh and Glasgow, leaving Euston Station by 10.0 a.m. Down Express, and returning from Edinburgh and Glasgow by 10.0 a.m. Up Express on Week Days. *NO EXTRA CHARGE* is made for Passengers travelling in these Saloons, and Compartments are specially reserved for Ladies and Family Parties.

SLEEPING SALOONS,

Provided with Pillows, Rugs, and Lavatory Accommodation, and Lighted with Gas,

Between London and Perth and Glasgow, and CARRIAGES with SLEEPING COMPARTMENTS are also run between London and Edinburgh and Greenock by the Night Trains. The extra charge for berths in the Saloons or Sleeping Carriages is 5s. in addition to the ordinary 1st class fare.

Conductors, in charge of the Luggage, &c., travel by the Through Trains. Dog Boxes specially provided.

Game Consignments conveyed by the Limited Mail.

OMNIBUSES capable of carrying *Six persons inside and Two outside*, with the usual quantity of Luggage, are provided *to meet Trains at Euston Station* when previously ordered. The Omnibuses will also be sent to any *Hotels or Private Residences* for conveyance to Euston Station of parties proposing to travel by the WEST COAST ROUTE. Application to be made to the Station-master at Euston Station.

Passengers from Scotland, by the WEST COAST ROUTE, travelling by the Limited Mail, or other Through Scotch Trains from Perth, Glasgow, Edinburgh, and Stations South, can secure these Omnibuses to meet the Trains, on arrival at Euston Station, by giving notice to the respective Station-masters before starting.

On application being made at Perth or any of the intermediate Stations between Perth and London, a telegraph message will be sent to the Station-master at Euston should an Omnibus be required to meet the Limited Mail due at Euston at 4.5 a.m.

The 'Buses can *generally* be obtained on arrival of the Train at Euston, even though not previously ordered.

Passengers are requested to ask for Tickets by the
WEST COAST ROUTE.

For full particulars of Train Service, Tourist Arrangements, &c., see the L. & N.-W. and Caledonian Coy.'s Time Books, or West Coast Tourist Guide, which can be obtained at all principal Stations.

June, 1882.   BY ORDER.

THE GUN OF THE FUTURE.

S. W. SILVER & CO.'S
Hammerless Gun.

Price from £15 15s.

FITTED WITH SILVER'S PATENT TRULY AUTOMATIC SAFETY BOLT.

The act of loading effectually secures both Tumblers and Triggers; these are released only when the Gun is in position for firing. Immediately the Gun is taken from the shoulder the Locks become automatically blocked.

The Safety Bolt can be applied to any kind of Hammerless Gun now in use.

PRESS NOTICES, ETC.

"The only system that can claim to be truly automatic."

"**F. R. M.,**" Letter to "**The Field.**"

PRESS NOTICES—*continued.*

"Out-and-out the safest gun ever yet brought out; the more I see it the better I like it."
"20,000 Shots at Marks," Letter to "The Field."

"In most guns the normal state is danger; in Silver's the normal state is safety."
"Vanity Fair."

"The gun is unlocked from safety simply by the fact of the shooter pressing the stock with his right hand when firing."
"Exchange and Mart."

"It renders the securing of the sportsman against danger from his gun altogether independent of his own will, and in this respect, as its name implies, the bolt is truly automatic."
"Morning Advertiser."

"In Messrs. Silver's gun the great drawback to the 'Hammerless' type has been obviated by a strictly automatic arrangement."
"European Mail."

"The action is so completely automatic and safe that the weapon cannot be discharged except when the shooter is ready and desirous of doing so."
"Land and Water."

New Illustrated Catalogue, with full particulars of above, and of every article of Equipment for Sportsmen, Colonists, Settlers, Explorers, and Travellers, on application to

S. W. SILVER & CO.,
67, CORNHILL, LONDON.

KYNOCH & CO.,
AMMUNITION MANUFACTURERS,
MILITARY AND SPORTING CARTRIDGES,
PERCUSSION CAPS, FOG SIGNALS for RAILWAYS.

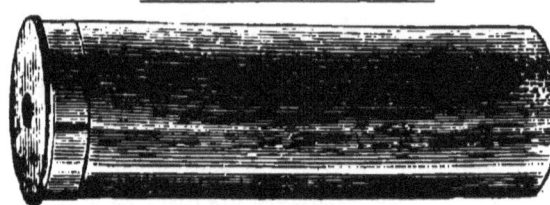

"Perfect" Case Empty.

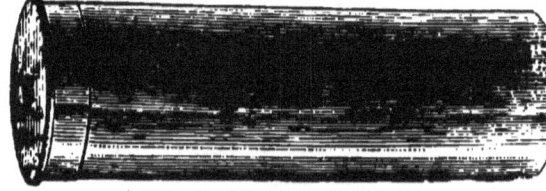

"Perfect" Case Loaded.

THE CHEAPEST CARTRIDGE IN THE TRADE.

KYNOCH & CO. beg to draw the attention of Sportsmen, Merchants, Gunmakers, &c. to this New Cartridge, which possesses the following advantages:

1st.—**Extra Regularity and Strength in Shooting.**
2nd.—**Increased Room for Powder.** Doing away with weakness of barrel caused by long chambers when heavy charges are required.
3rd.—**Damp Proof.** They are not affected by wet, consequently there is no difficulty either in inserting or extracting.
4th.—**Weight is less than the Paper Cartridge.**
5th.—**Cheapness.**—The Price is the same as the "Green Gas-tight." As the shells are of considerable value after being used, the original cost will be reduced to the same as the cheapest brown cartridge.
6th.—The case is specially adapted for Schultze Powder.
7th.—**Pigeon Shooting.**—The first six gentlemen who used these cartridges won their matches.

KYNOCH'S (Green, Blue, and Brown, also Salmon for Schultze Powder) PAPER SPORTING CARTRIDGES in every size.
KYNOCH'S SOLID METAL MARTINI-HENRY CARTRIDGES.
KYNOCH'S SOLID METAL EXPRESS CARTRIDGES.
KYNOCH'S NICKEL PLATED SPORTING CARTRIDGES.
KYNOCH'S SOLID METAL AND PAPER PUNT GUN CARTRIDGES.
KYNOCH'S ROOK-RIFLE CARTRIDGES.
KYNOCH'S REVOLVER CARTRIDGES.

Illustrated Catalogue, Price List, and Samples forwarded to Merchants or Gunmakers on application to

KYNOCH & CO., WITTON, near BIRMINGHAM.

THE INTERNATIONAL FUR STORE,

163 and 165, REGENT STREET, LONDON, W.

THE CHEAPEST HOUSE IN LONDON FOR HIGH-CLASS FURS.

SPECIALTIES—

LADIES' SEALSKIN COATS,
FUR-LINED CLOAKS,
HATS, MUFFS, BAGS, &c.,
AND
MEN'S FUR COATS AND RUGS.

TERMS CASH. ALL GOODS MARKED IN PLAIN FIGURES.

Fur Garments of all descriptions Repaired and Remodelled by experienced Workmen.

RAW SKINS PREPARED AND MOUNTED.

ESTIMATES GIVEN.

THE INTERNATIONAL FUR STORE,

REGENT STREET, LONDON, W.

T. S. JAY, Manager.

House Furnishing and Decorating.

CONRATH & SONS,

15 and 40, NORTH AUDLEY STREET, Grosvenor Square, W.,

Invite special attention to the character of their old-established Business, which is conducted on the lines of excellence and economy, at their newly-erected Manufactory. All the work is closely supervised by themselves personally, thereby ensuring to the purchaser the lowest cost of production, combined with sound construction and true design.

SPECIALTIES IN
SUITES FOR SHOOTING & HUNTING LODGES.

DINING-ROOM SETS,
In Walnut, Ash, and other Hard Woods, Twenty-five Pounds.

BED-ROOM SETS,
IN DURABLE WOODS, FROM FIFTEEN POUNDS.

ANTIQUE FURNITURE.
CONRATH & SONS have Special Reputation for dealing in Genuine Specimens at Moderate Prices.

Carpets, Curtain Materials, Wall-hangings, and Decorations
Of the most approved styles, English, Continental, and Oriental.

SPECIAL AGENTS FOR
THE LINCRUSTA WALTON DECORATION.

Estimates and Catalogues Free to all parts of the Country.

ESTATE AGENCY DEPARTMENT.
A very extensive Register of Town and Country Properties for disposal forwarded on application.

CONRATH & SONS,
15 & 40, North Audley Street, Grosvenor Square, W.
Manufactory: UXBRIDGE ROAD, W.

THE LATEST IMPROVEMENT.

SPRATTS PATENT

Meat "Fibrine" Vegetable

DOG CAKES

(WITH BEETROOT—IMPROVED PATENT).

USED IN THE ROYAL KENNELS. BEWARE OF WORTHLESS IMITATIONS:

Please see that every Cake is stamped "Spratts Patent," and a "X."

PUPPY FOOD.

PRICE 3s. PER TIN.

REARS PUPPIES FROM BIRTH.

Highly recommended by "The Field."

BONE MEAL FOR PUPPIES.

Finely granulated and specially prepared.

PRICE 1s. PER TIN.

GAME MEAL AND "CRISSEL."

THE MOST SUCCESSFUL FOODS FOR
REARING PHEASANTS AND ALL KINDS OF GAME.

POULTRY MEAL.

REARS CHICKS, TURKEYS, AND DUCKLINGS FROM THE SHELL WITH THE MINIMUM OF LOSS.

"SPRATTS PATENT," BERMONDSEY, S.E.

HUNTING QUARTERS.

ROYAL GEORGE
HOTEL,
RUGBY.

One of the Best Houses in the Midlands.

GOOD CUISINE, WINE, AND ATTENDANCE.

TABLE D'HOTE DURING THE HUNTING SEASON.

TARIFF.   *NIGHT PORTER.*

GOOD STABLING.   POSTING.

SPORTING WORKS

BY

FRED. FIELD WHITEHURST

("A VETERAN").

Each in One Vol., crown 8vo, cloth, price Nine Shillings.

ON THE GRAMPIAN HILLS: Grouse and Ptarmigan Shooting, Deer Stalking, Salmon and Trout Fishing, &c. By FRED. FIELD WHITEHURST ("A Veteran"), Author of "Tally-Ho!" "Harkaway," &c.

A Goodly Gathering, The Coaching Club, The Four-in-Hand Club, Society in the Saddle, Riders in the Row, &c.

HARKAWAY: Sketches of Hunting, Coaching, Fishing, &c. By FRED. FIELD WHITEHURST ("A Veteran"), Author of "Tally-Ho!" &c.

"It is just the book for a country-house smoking-room, and is sure to prove a favourite."—*World.*

"Remarkable for their freshness and vigour."—*Court Journal.*

A Day with the Baron, The Four-in-Hand Club, A Year's Coachings, A Forest Run with "The Queen's," Hunting the Wild Red Deer, The Royal Buckhounds, A Pink Wedding; Melton, its Manners and Customs; &c.

TALLY-HO! Sketches of Hunting, Coaching, &c. By FRED. FIELD WHITEHURST ("A Veteran").

"The sketches are full of life and spirit, and we doubt not lovers of the chase will be glad to read a description of the famous runs recorded in the present volume."—*Court Journal.*

"Many a hard rider will recognise in these pages a faithful picture of runs in which he has himself figured with distinction."—*Man of the World.*

"A very agreeable book, calculated to be a good companion to hunting-men."—*Sporting Gazette.*

TINSLEY BROTHERS, 8, CATHERINE STREET, STRAND.

NEW BOOKS FOR THE SEASON.

ON THE GRAMPIAN HILLS: Grouse and Ptarmigan Shooting, Deer Stalking, Salmon and Trout Fishing, &c. By FRED. FIELD WHITEHURST ("A Veteran"), Author of "Tally-Ho!" "Harkaway." 1 vol. 9s.

ROAD SCRAPINGS: Coaches and Coaching. By MARTIN E. HAWORTH, late Captain 60th Rifles, Queen's Foreign Service Messenger, M.F.H., &c., Author of "The Silver Greyhound." 1 vol. 8vo. With 12 Coloured Illustrations. 10s. 6d.

MEN WE MEET IN THE FIELD; or, The Bullshire Hounds. By A. G. BAGOT ("Bagatelle"), Author of "Sporting Sketches in Three Continents," &c. 1 vol. 7s. 6d.

TALES AND TRADITIONS OF SWITZERLAND. By WILLIAM WESTALL, Author of "Larry Lohengrin," "The Old Factory," &c. 1 vol. crown 8vo. 10s. 6d.

NEW WORKS OF TRAVEL.

WITH A SHOW THROUGH SOUTHERN AFRICA, and Personal Reminiscences of the Transvaal War. By CHARLES DU VAL, late of the Carabineers, Attaché to the Staff of Garrison Commandant, and Editor of the *News of the Camp* during the investment of Pretoria. 1 vol. demy 8vo. With numerous Illustrations.

PALMS AND TEMPLES: Incidents of a Four Months' Voyage on the Nile. With Notes upon the Antiquities, Scenery, People, and Sport of Egypt. By JULIAN B. ARNOLD. Prefatory Notice by EDWIN ARNOLD, Author of "The Light of Asia," &c. 1 vol. demy 8vo. With Frontispiece and Vignette. 12s.

AMONG THE SONS OF HAN: Notes of a Six Years' Residence in China and Formosa. By Mrs. T. F. HUGHES. 1 vol. demy 8vo. With Map. 12s.

KEANE'S JOURNEYS TO MECCAH & MEDINAH. Each in 1 vol. demy 8vo. 10s. 6d.

TINSLEY BROTHERS, 8, CATHERINE STREET, STRAND.

"GOLD LACK" CHAMPAGNE,

SHIPPED BY

DEUTZ & GELDERMANN.

THE WINE FOR PRINCES AND SENATORS.

The district of Ay has become probably the most celebrated in the ancient province of Champagne for its grapes, and among the famous brands of that famed region, not one has gained a popularity to a greater extent in this country than that of DEUTZ & GELDERMANN. The Wine of this well-known firm is invariably met with on every important occasion, and it is noticed that DEUTZ & GELDERMANN's "Gold Lack" was specially selected for the Banquet given by the Royal Naval Club at Portsmouth to H. R. H. the Prince of Wales, and some proof of its excellence may be gathered from the fact that this brand was drunk on a former visit of the Prince to the club two years since. DEUTZ & GELDERMANN's "Gold Lack" was one of the Champagnes supplied at the late Ministerial Whitebait dinner at the Trafalgar.—*Morning Post.*

The "GOLD LACK," Sec or Extra Sec, can be obtained from all Wine Merchants.

www.ingramcontent.com/pod-product-compliance
Lightning Source LLC
Chambersburg PA
CBHW032008230426
43672CB00010B/2290